ACOUSTIC
GUITAR
private
lessons

D1399572

MUSIC BASICS
FOR GUITARISTS

Learn the Fundamentals of Music Theory,
Chord Progressions, Scales, Notation, and More

by the Master Teachers at *Acoustic Guitar*

STRING LETTER PUBLISHING

Publisher: David A. Lusterman

Editor: Jeffrey Pepper Rodgers

Group Publisher and Editorial Director: Dan Gabel

Music Editor and Engraver: Andrew DuBrock

Art Director: Barbara Summer

Design and Production: Kristin Wallace

Cover Photograph: Barbara Summer

© 2010 String Letter Publishing

ISBN 978-1-890490-71-3

Printed in the United States of America

This book was produced by String Letter Publishing, Inc.

PO Box 767, San Anselmo, CA 94979-0767

(415) 485-6946; StringLetter.com

Library of Congress Cataloging-in-Publication Data

Music basics for guitarists : learn the fundamentals of music theory, chord progressions, scales, notation, and more / by the master teachers at Acoustic guitar.

    p. cm. -- (Acoustic guitar private lessons)

Includes bibliographical references and index.

ISBN 978-1-890490-71-3 (alk. paper)

1. Music--Instruction and study. 2. Music theory. I. Acoustic guitar.

  MT584.M87 2010

  781.2--dc22

                2010045720

STRING LETTER PUBLISHING

CONTENTS

INTRODUCTION **4**

CD Track No.   1   Tune-Up

UNDERSTAND NOTATION

MUSIC NOTATION 101 Andrew DuBrock **5**

2   **TAB READING TIPS** David Hodge **9**
6   *Once I Had a Sweetheart* **12**

7   **START READING MUSIC** Sean McGowan **14**

16   **DECODING CHORD SYMBOLS** Dan Apczynski **18**

25   **THE FUNDAMENTALS OF TIME** Ruth Parry **24**
33   *Paint by Rhythms* **29**

CHORDS AND PROGRESSIONS

34   **DIATONIC CHORDS** Dan Apczynski **30**
39   *Dye and Tonic* **34**

40   **THE CIRCLE OF FIFTHS** Adam Perlmutter **35**
44   *Pickin' in Circles* **38**

45   **THE C-A-G-E-D SYSTEM** Dan Apczynski **39**
51   *Uncaged Melody* **42**

52   **TRANSPOSING MADE EASY** David Hodge **43**
58   *Broke and Hungry* **46**

SCALES AND MODES

61   **THE MAJOR SCALE** Andrew DuBrock **49**
74   *Mostly Major Melody* **54**

75   **MINOR KEYS** Andrew DuBrock **55**
79   *Carolan's Welcome* **58**

80   **PENTATONIC SCALES** Adam Perlmutter **61**
88   *All Pent Up* **65**

89   **UNDERSTANDING MODES** Adam Levy **66**

ABOUT THE TEACHERS **71**

INTRODUCTION

Like so many guitarists, I learned to play mostly by ear—spinning favorite tracks and slowly, by trial and error, figuring out how to reproduce or at least approximate the guitar parts. Only later did I begin to work with written notation and piece together the logic behind the music so that I could understand, for instance, what makes an Em7 an Em7, why that chord fits so well in a song in the key of G, and which scale I can use to solo over it. The best thing about this kind of information is that it makes knowledge of the guitar transportable. You can discover a cool sound in one place on the fingerboard and quickly figure out how to play it in a different position or key, or you can take an idea from one song and apply it to another. Instead of just memorizing where to put your fingers, you can see the underlying patterns and use them in other contexts. In addition, music theory presents you with options that your fingers may not know yet—it's a road map for places you can travel.

This book breaks down the basics of music theory into easy-to-follow lessons designed specifically for guitarists. The first section is a primer on reading guitar notation, and then

the lessons proceed through the basics of understanding chords, chord progressions, scales, and modes—the building blocks of songs and solos. Throughout, the teachers provide examples (on the page and on the accompanying CD) that show the theory at work in real music—which is the point, after all. With a little woodshedding on basic theory, you'll find new ways for the brain, fingers, and ears to work together and open up new possibilities and sounds on your guitar.

Happy playing.

—*Jeffrey Pepper Rodgers*

CD **TRACK 1** **Introduction and Tune-up**

MUSIC NOTATION 101

Andrew DuBrock

Reading music is no different than reading a book. In both cases, you need to understand the language that you're reading; you can't read Chinese characters if you don't understand them, and you can't read music if you don't understand the written symbols behind music notation.

Guitarists use several types of notation, including standard notation, tablature, and chord grids. Standard notation is the main notation system common to all instruments and styles in Western music. Knowing standard notation will allow you to share and play music with almost any other instrument. Tablature is a notation system exclusively for stringed instruments with frets—like guitar and mandolin—that shows you what strings and frets to play at any given moment. Chord grids use a graphic representation of the fretboard to show chord shapes for fretted stringed instruments. Here's a primer on how to read these types of notation.

Standard Notation

Standard notation is written on a five-line staff. Notes are written in alphabetical order from A to G. Every time you pass a G note, the sequence of notes repeats—starting with A.

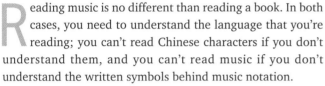

The duration of a note is determined by three things: the note head, stem, and flag. A whole note (𝅝) equals four beats. A half note (𝅗𝅥) is half of that: two beats. A quarter note (♩) equals one beat, an eighth note (♪) equals half of one beat, and a 16th note (𝅘𝅥𝅯) is a quarter beat (there are four 16th notes per beat).

The fraction (4/4, 3/4, 6/8, etc.) or 𝄴 character shown at the beginning of a piece of music denotes the time signature. The top number tells you how many beats are in each measure, and the bottom number indicates the rhythmic value of each beat (4 equals a quarter note, 8 equals an eighth note, 16 equals a 16th note, and 2 equals a half note).

The most common time signature is 4/4, which signifies four quarter notes per measure and is sometimes designated with the symbol 𝄴 (for common time). The symbol 𝄵 stands for cut time (2/2). Most songs are either in 4/4 or 3/4.

Tablature

In tablature, the six horizontal lines represent the six strings of the guitar, with the first string on the top and sixth on the bottom. The numbers refer to fret numbers on a given string.

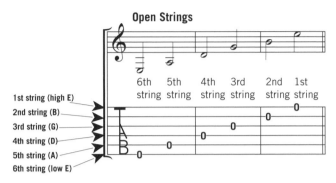

The notation and tablature in this book are designed to be used in tandem—refer to the notation to get the rhythmic information and note durations, and refer to the tablature to get the exact locations of the notes on the guitar fingerboard.

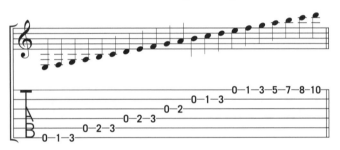

Fingerings

Fingerings are indicated with small numbers and letters in the notation. Fretting-hand fingering is indicated with 1 for the index finger, 2 the middle, 3 the ring, 4 the pinky, and *T* the thumb. Picking-hand fingering is indicated by *i* for the index finger, *m* the middle, *a* the ring, *c* the pinky, and *p* the thumb. Circled numbers indicate the string the note is played on. Remember that the fingerings indicated are only suggestions; if you find a different way that works better for you, use it.

Strumming and Picking

In music played with a flatpick, downstrokes (toward the floor) and upstrokes (toward the ceiling) are shown as follows. Slashes in the notation and tablature indicate a strum through the previously played chord.

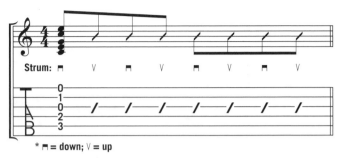

* ⊓ = down; ∨ = up

In music played with the pick-hand fingers, *split stems* are often used to highlight the division between thumb and fingers. With split stems, notes played by the thumb have stems pointing down, while notes played by the fingers have stems pointing up. If split stems are not used, pick-hand fingerings are usually present. Here is the same fingerpicking pattern shown with and without split stems.

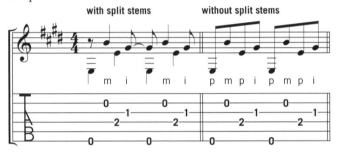

Chord Diagrams

Chord diagrams show where the fingers go on the fingerboard. Frets are shown horizontally. The thick top line represents the nut. A fret number to the right of a diagram indicates a chord played higher up the neck (in this case the top horizontal line is thin). Strings are shown as vertical lines. The line on the far left represents the sixth (lowest) string, and the line on the far right represents the first (highest) string. Dots show where the fingers go, and thick horizontal lines indicate barres. Numbers above the diagram are left-hand finger numbers, as used in standard notation.

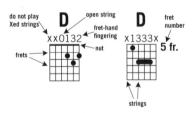

Again, the fingerings are only suggestions. An *X* indicates a string that should be muted or not played; 0 indicates an open string.

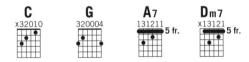

6

Capos

If a capo is used, a Roman numeral indicates the fret where the capo should be placed. The standard notation and tablature is written as if the capo were the nut of the guitar. For instance, a tune capoed anywhere up the neck and played using key-of-G chord shapes and fingerings will be written in the key of G. Likewise, open strings held down by the capo are written as open strings.

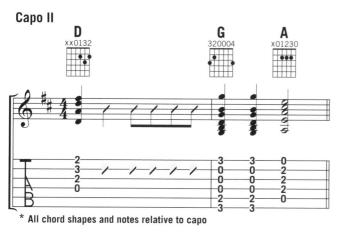

* All chord shapes and notes relative to capo

Tunings

Alternate guitar tunings are given from the lowest (sixth) string to the highest (first) string. For instance, D A D G B E indicates standard tuning with the bottom string dropped to D. Standard notation for songs in alternate tunings always reflects the actual pitches of the notes. Arrows underneath tuning notes indicate strings that are altered from standard tuning and whether they are tuned up or down.

Tuning: D A D G B E

Vocal Tunes

Vocal tunes are sometimes written with a fully tabbed-out introduction and a vocal melody with chord diagrams for the rest of the piece. The tab intro is usually your indication of which strum or fingerpicking pattern to use in the rest of the piece. The melody with lyrics underneath is the melody sung by the vocalist. Occasionally, smaller notes are written with the melody to indicate other instruments or the harmony part sung by another vocalist. These are not to be confused with cue notes, which are small notes that indicate melodies that vary when a section is repeated. Listen to a recording of the piece to get a feel for the guitar accompaniment and to hear the singing if you aren't skilled at reading vocal melodies.

You've got to move

Articulations

There are a number of ways you can articulate a note on the guitar. Notes connected with slurs (not to be confused with ties) in the tablature or standard notation are articulated with either a hammer-on, pull-off, or slide. Lower notes slurred to higher notes are played as hammer-ons; higher notes slurred to lower notes are played as pull-offs. While it's usually obvious that slurred notes are played as hammer-ons or pull-offs, an *H* or *P* is included above the tablature as an extra reminder.

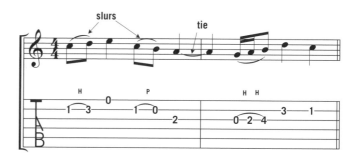

Slides are represented with a dash, and an *S* is included above the tab. A dash preceding a note represents a slide into the note from an indefinite point in the direction of the slide; a dash following a note indicates a slide off of the note to an indefinite point in the direction of the slide. For two slurred notes connected with a slide, you should pick the first note and then slide into the second.

Bends are represented with upward curves, as shown in the next example. Most bends have a specific destination pitch—the number above the bend symbol shows how much the bend raises the string's pitch: ¼ for a slight bend, ½ for a half step, 1 for a whole step.

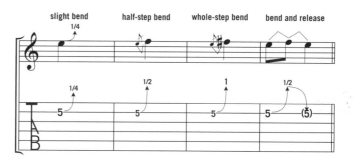

Grace notes are represented by small notes with a dash through the stem in standard notation and with small numbers in the tab. A grace note is a very quick ornament leading into a note, most commonly executed as a hammer-on, pull-off, or slide. In the first example below, pluck the note at the fifth fret on the beat, then quickly hammer onto the seventh fret. The second example is executed as a quick pull-off from the second fret to the open string. In the third example, both notes at the fifth fret are played simultaneously (even though it appears that the fifth fret, fourth string, is to be played by itself), then the seventh fret, fourth string, is quickly hammered.

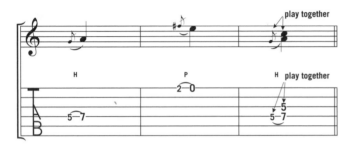

Harmonics

Harmonics are represented by diamond-shaped notes in the standard notation and a small dot next to the tablature numbers. Natural harmonics are indicated with the text "Harmonics" or "Harm." above the tablature. Harmonics articulated with the right hand (often called artificial harmonics) include the text "R.H. Harmonics" or "R.H. Harm." above the tab. Right-hand harmonics are executed by lightly touching the harmonic node (usually 12 frets above the open string or fretted note) with the right-hand index finger and plucking the string with the thumb or ring finger or pick. For extended phrases played with right-hand harmonics, the fretted notes are shown in the tab along with instructions to touch the harmonics 12 frets above the notes.

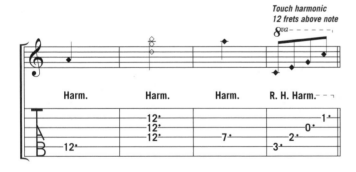

Repeats

One of the most confusing parts of a musical score can be the navigation symbols, such as repeats, *D.S. al Coda*, *D.C. al Fine*, *To Coda*, etc. Repeat symbols are placed at the beginning and end of the passage to be repeated.

You should ignore repeat symbols with the dots on the right side the first time you encounter them; when you come to a repeat symbol with dots on the left side, jump back to the previous repeat symbol facing the opposite direction (if there is no previous symbol, go to the beginning of the piece). The next time you come to the repeat symbol, ignore it and keep going unless it includes instructions such as "Repeat three times."

A section will often have a different ending after each repeat. The example below includes a first and a second ending. Play until you hit the repeat symbol, jump back to the previous repeat symbol and play until you reach the bracketed first ending, skip the measures under the bracket and jump immediately to the second ending, and then continue.

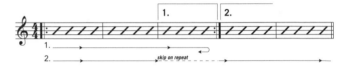

D.S. stands for *dal segno* or "from the sign." When you encounter this indication, jump immediately to the sign (𝄋). *D.S.* is usually accompanied by *al Fine* or *al Coda*. Fine indicates the end of a piece. A coda is a final passage near the end of a piece and is indicated with ⊕. *D.S. al Coda* simply tells you to jump back to the sign and continue on until you are instructed to jump to the coda, indicated with *To Coda* ⊕.

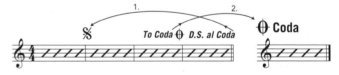

D.C. stands for *da capo* or "from the beginning." Jump to the top of the piece when you encounter this indication.

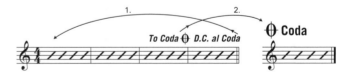

D.C. al Fine tells you to jump to the beginning of a tune and continue until you encounter the *Fine* indicating the end of the piece (ignore the *Fine* the first time through).

TAB READING TIPS

David Hodge

We guitarists love tablature; many players claim that they couldn't have learned how to play the guitar without it. As a teacher, though, I've found that many people who only read tablature have some habits that can actually hinder them from becoming better players. They often don't know the notes they are playing and can't recognize basic chord shapes, even when the notes in those chords are tabbed out.

People who have learned to read music of polyphonic instruments (which play more than one note at a time—such as the guitar and piano) usually develop the ability to read music in different directions. Not only do they read left to right, they also read up and down. They also take in notes in *groups* and *phrases*. These skills allow the guitarist to see chords in the notation, as well as lead lines or little riffs and fills.

Many beginners read tablature one number (tabbed note) at a time, even when looking at chords that have been tabbed out. But, with a little time and practice, you should be able to look at, say, **Example 1** and recognize it as an A7 chord without a second thought. Let's see if we can't get you on your way to doing just that.

Find Familiar Faces

The first step toward developing a big-picture outlook in reading tablature is to recognize chord shapes. This starts with open-position chords, as shown in **Example 2**. Now, it's one thing to be able to recognize a chord when it's all nicely lined up, but guitar music, especially acoustic-guitar music, often uses arpeggios and different fingerpicking patterns. **Example 3** is an open-position D-major chord, although it might take you a moment to see this. Learning to take in this whole measure (or at least the first five notes) at a glance will help you to recognize a chord shape even when it's spread out over an arpeggio.

Make your tab reading more efficient—and your playing more enjoyable—by learning to see groups and phrases, as you would in standard notation.

Sometimes, though, it can be tricky. The first measure of **Example 4** is also a D-major chord, but it has some frills added, namely adding the G note (third fret of the first string), which momentarily makes it a Dsus4 chord. The second measure of this example demonstrates a "broken chord" strumming pattern. Simply taking in this entire measure at once, you should be able to see that it's still nothing but a D-major chord.

Trickier still is recognizing these shapes further up the neck. A riff such as the one in **Example 5** starts with an open D-major shape, but it's played up at the seventh fret. The big clue in this example is the "7, 8, 7" descending arpeggio of the second, third, and fourth notes. That's your D-major shape, moved up the neck to create a G-major chord.

As with most things about the guitar, being able to see these shapes in tablature becomes easier with practice. But it's the kind of practice where you have to bring your brain as well as your fingers. In **Example 6** you will see a partial chord riff based on the E-major-shaped barre chord of A. See if you can pick out the telltale signs.

Double-stop leads and fills—where you play two notes at the same time—become a snap when you start getting more comfortable reading tablature in terms of shapes rather than numbers. **Example 7** gives you an example of a typical double-stop riff that employs the familiar open-chord shapes of E, A, and D.

Dig for Phrases

Another good tablature reading habit to develop is looking at the music in terms of phrases, especially for lead or riff-based rhythm guitar. Not only will this help you get better at recognizing your tablature-written chord shapes, it will also give you some vital clues with regard to finger placement.

Phrases are easier to discern when read as notation: You can see the physical groups or clusters of notes, even if you don't know what the notes are. Picking apart a phrase written in tablature usually involves looking at a specific area of the fingerboard. Look for groups of notes written within a two-to-four-fret span of each other, such as those in **Example 8**. Here you can see two distinct phrases: one in the first measure,

Ex. 4
(continued)

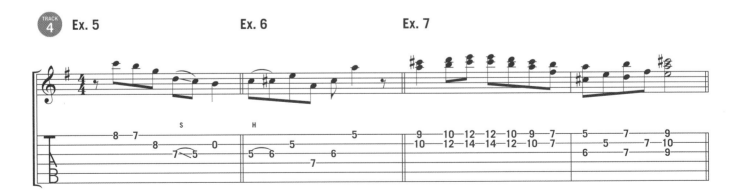

Ex. 5   **Ex. 6**   **Ex. 7**

which takes place between the third and fifth frets, and one in the second measure that is played between the seventh and tenth frets.

A good (but not foolproof) rule of thumb is to look for the lowest fret number of your phrase. If you think of planting your index finger at the lowest fret of the phrase, chances are pretty good that this will lead you to determine the correct chord shape to use in playing the phrase.

Remember, too, that many guitar phrases are based on what's called "the box." A box is usually a span of two frets across the middle strings of your instrument. **Example 9** shows a box-based riff. Again, using your index finger for the lowest-numbered fret (in this particular example, the fifth fret) will usually set you up well for playing the rest of the phrase.

Try a Song

This big-picture approach is especially useful when reading chord melodies written out in tablature. For this lesson I've included **"Once I Had a Sweetheart,"** a traditional Appalachian folksong, to give you a little test of your new skills. This isn't a fancy arrangement—it involves very basic partial chords and fingerings—but it provides examples of each of the ideas we've covered.

As a teacher, I'm often asked whether it's better to know music notation or tablature. Frankly, I don't see why this should be an either/or choice. Both systems of reading music can benefit guitarists enormously. But whichever system you choose to help you with your music, it's important to make the most of it. Applying some of the tips covered in this lesson to your reading of tablature should help make your guitar playing more facile—and more enjoyable.

TRACK 5 · Ex. 8 · Ex. 9

Once I Had a Sweetheart

Traditional, arranged by David Hodge

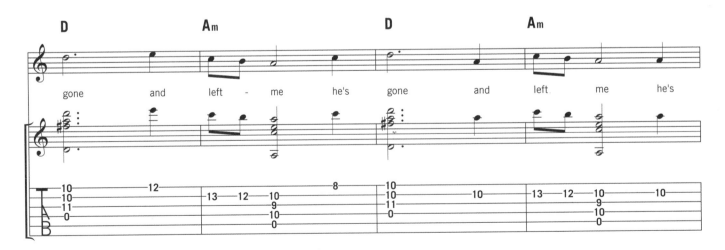

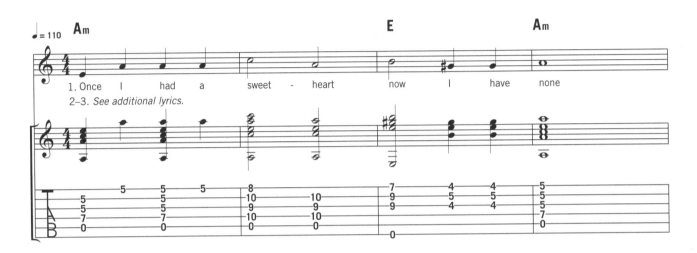

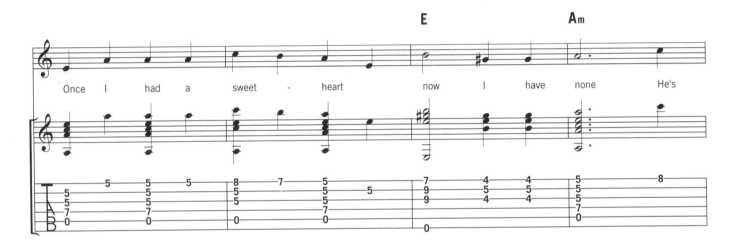

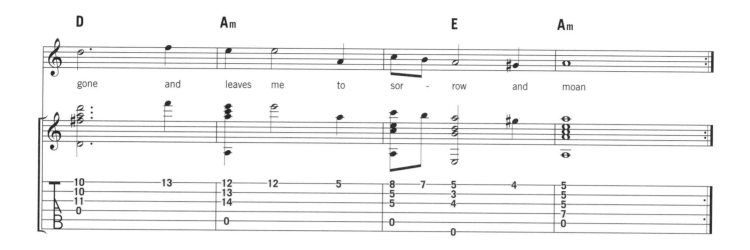

gone   and   leaves   me   to   sor - row   and   moan

Am   E   Am
1.   Once I had a sweetheart, now I have none

Am   E   Am
Once I had a sweetheart, now I have none

    D   Am   D   Am
He's gone and left me, he's gone and left me

    D   Am   E   Am
He's gone and leaves me to sorrow and moan

Am   E   Am
2.   Last night in sweet slumber, I dreamed I did see

Am   E   Am
Last night in sweet slumber, I dreamed I did see

    D   Am   D   Am
My own darling jewel sat smiling by me

    D   Am   E   Am
My own darling jewel sat smiling by me

Am   E   Am
3.   But when I awakened, I found it not so

Am   E   Am
But when I awakened, I found it not so

    D   Am   D   Am
My eyes, like some fountain, with tears overflowed

    D   Am   E Am
My eyes, like some fountain, with tears overflowed

START READING MUSIC

Sean McGowan

There's a common joke told among musicians: "How do you get a guitarist to lower his volume?" The answer: "Give him some sheet music." It's a bit of a stereotype, but the truth is that many guitarists don't read standard music notation—it's just not a big part of guitar culture (compared to, say, piano culture). Many bands don't use sheet music, most guitar music is available in tablature, and few guitar teachers require that their students read music unless they're in an advanced music program. Despite all this, guitarists can really benefit from time spent learning to read and play from standard notation. A few compelling reasons include a deeper understanding of music and the guitar fretboard, a means of communicating with other musicians, the ability to take gigs and work in a variety of styles that do use sheet music, and most important, access to incredible music written for other instruments in all styles.

> Learn to understand the language of music by breaking the goal into half-hour practice sessions.

Learning to read is not as difficult as many guitarists seem to think. It is possible to learn to read at a high level on the guitar, and it's important to recognize that it doesn't take hours a day to learn to read competently. In fact, it's much more important to practice reading a little every day rather than once a week for, say, three hours at a time.

In this lesson, we've created a 30-minute workout that can help you isolate the fundamentals of reading music, including the ability to recognize the pitches and rhythms of printed music and simultaneously locate and articulate the correct pitches on the fretboard.

Know Your Pitches: 5 Minutes

The first (and easiest) thing any musician needs to do to start reading music is to become familiar with the notes of the staff. A music staff is made up of horizontal lines and the spaces between them, and each one corresponds to a different pitch. Perhaps you're already aware of the mnemonic device "every good boy does fine"—a system of remembering which pitches correspond to the lines of the treble staff (from low to high): E–G–B–D–F (**Example 1**). The spaces between the lines spell the word F–A–C–E (**Example 2**).

A good first exercise is to create a pitch chart and practice naming the notes. Take a blank sheet of staff paper and fill

TRACK 7 Ex. 1   Ex. 2

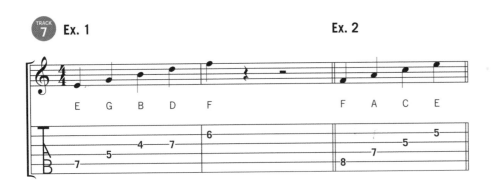

every staff randomly with quarter notes. Do not use any sharps or flats and start with smaller skips (**Example 3**). You can make each pitch collection more difficult by spreading out the intervals (**Example 4**). Here's how to practice: first, simply say the names of each pitch in time with a metronome. Do this at a comfortable tempo—you may need to start very slowly. It's very important not to go too fast, and to keep your place in the music, especially when moving to another staff. Practice looking ahead of the pitch you are naming and stay in time! After you've finished working through your pitch chart, go back and repeat by simultaneously saying the pitches aloud and playing them on your guitar. When you feel like you're starting to memorize the pitches instead of reading them off the page, simply turn your sheet of staff paper upside-down and you'll have a brand-new pitch chart!

Note that the guitar is actually an octave-transposing instrument; our pitches sound an octave lower than other instruments. For example, the guitar's middle C (the note that appears on the first line below the treble staff) is played on the third fret of the A string (**Example 5**), while a "universal" middle C—the middle C in a piece of piano music—sounds one octave higher (**Example 6**). If it helps you get your bearings, another good rule of thumb is that the G on the second line of the staff (the "good" in E–G–B–D–F) is equal to the open G string in standard tuning.

Feel the Rhythm: 10 minutes

The next element to focus on is the duration of various notes—the amount of time each note is held before moving on to the next one. Let's keep it simple and work on basic phrases that use simple patterns. These examples are all in 4/4 time—the most common time signature in Western music—which basically means that each quarter note gets one beat, and that there are four beats in each measure. Set your

TRACK 8 **Ex. 3**

Ex. 4

TRACK 9 **Ex. 5**   **Ex. 6**

metronome to a slow tempo in 4/4 time and count the quarter notes in **Example 7** along with each click. The half notes in **Example 8** are twice as long as quarter notes, so each one gets two clicks (or half of a measure). The eighth notes in **Example 9** are twice as fast as quarter notes, counted "one-and two-and three-and four-and." When you encounter a piece of music that includes notes and rests (like **Example 10**), keep counting in time. Remember, music encompasses sound and silence, but the rhythm never stops. Try practicing Example 10 by clapping the rhythm along with the metronome while counting the notes aloud. If you can't quite figure out how it's supposed to sound, check out the CD tracks.

Find It, Play It: 15 minutes

Perhaps the hardest part of reading for guitarists is figuring out where to play each note on the fretboard. Our third exercise involves practicing note location. Try this: name any note and see how quickly you can find it on each string. Next, try seeing where different notes are located in fifth position. If you've never tried this before, you'll probably find that it's a pretty difficult task!

Many guitarists learn to read notes in open position, however this can be restrictive in range. Starting in fifth position gives much more flexibility in range and timbre. Try reading your way through the pitch chart in **Example 11**, but keep your fretting hand in fifth position (only playing notes where they fall between the fifth and ninth frets). Doing this will give you more insight into the overall layout of the fretboard and a good starting point to extend that knowledge in either direction.

Create Your Own Rhythm Figures

It's not hard to create rhythm figures like the ones in Example 10. It's simple—each 4/4 measure should contain four beats. Count each quarter note or quarter rest as one beat, each half note or half rest as two, and each eighth note or eighth rest as one half. As long as the total of each measure adds up to exactly four beats, you're doing it right! There are other note durations to explore beyond quarter, half, and eighth notes, but these should provide a nice foundation and a good place to start writing your own simple rhythms.

Put It All Together

Once you start to feel familiar with the notes of the fretboard, you're ready to begin playing music right off the page. **Examples 12 to 16** use all of the concepts from this lesson to make nice, melodic exercises. If you're still hungry for more, there are a number of excellent books with reading études available; some guitarists even choose to work on melodies by using violin books and on rhythm by using snare drum studies. Remember, the key is to practice a short amount of time (30 minutes—pitches, rhythms, fretboard, and music) on a regular basis. Before you know it, you'll be reaping the rewards of reading!

DECODING CHORD SYMBOLS

Dan Apczynski

One of the best things about playing the guitar is how easy it is to get started—learn just a few basic chords and you're in business. Before long, though, you'll encounter a piece of music that requires more than those basic chords. It's OK to get a little frustrated—you certainly wouldn't be the first musician to get ticked off after seeing chord names with extra letters or numbers (and even shapes or arithmetic symbols).

The important thing is to recognize that these new chord symbols are not roadblocks; they're part of the learning process. With a little effort, they'll become part of your musical vocabulary and you'll be one step closer to being the guitar player you've always wanted to be. In this lesson, we'll look at a few of the chord symbols you're most likely to see, tell you what you need to know about them, and show you some fail-safe ways to play them.

No matter how simple or complicated they might appear, chord symbols are part of a classification system used by musicians. By giving chords names like "major," "minor," or "seventh" (among other things, and sometimes even a combination of these names), musicians know exactly what kind of chord is required and even the specific notes in the chord. In most cases, these words are abbreviated in the chord symbols used in written music.

Major and Minor Chords

If you're like most guitarists, *major* and *minor* chords were the first chords you learned, so it might seem strange that the words major and minor rarely appear in a written piece of music. That's because composers and transcribers use musical shorthand to convey these names in notation.

It's simpler than it sounds. For starters, every chord symbol you'll ever see starts with one capital letter, sometimes followed by a flat or sharp. The letter comes from a note called the *root;* the most important (and usually the lowest) note in the chord voicing. Major chords also include two other notes, called the *major third* and *fifth*, neither of which are called out by name in the chord symbol. Whenever you see a note name above a music staff with no other letters or numbers attached to it, the composer wants you to play a *major chord*. **Example 1** shows a few major chords in action. Experienced musicians sometimes call these chords by their full names ("A major," "D♭ major," etc.), but often they'll just use their letter names ("A," "D♭," etc.).

> Stuck on chord symbols that look like algebra problems? Use this simple guide to crack the code.

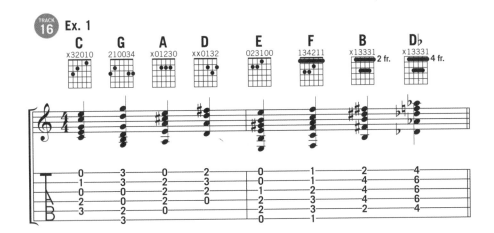

Ex. 1

Major chords are great because they're typically written the same way no matter what piece of music you're reading. But just about any other chord you're likely to come across could be written in several ways. Take minor chords, for example. In this book you will see chord names such as Em and F#m indicating minor chords. Like their major counterparts, these chords are named for the root notes upon which the chords are built (in this case, E and F#). Other publishers prefer to spell minor chords with different abbreviations. The abbreviation *min* is popular (as in Emin and F#min), and you might even see minor chords indicated with a minus symbol (as in E- and F#-). All these symbols mean the same thing. A few easy minor chords are shown in **Example 2**. Like major chords, minor chords include the root and fifth notes, but the third is lowered a half step (and usually referred to as the *flatted* or *minor third*).

Seventh Chords and Extensions

The major and minor chords in Examples 1 and 2 might seem like they're made up of four, five, or six notes, but the truth is that they're all built from only three notes (some of which are repeated at different octaves). Those three notes make up what are called *triads*. Seventh chords include a fourth note called a *seventh* (which, we admit, sounds paradoxical). Most seventh chords add this fourth note to regular major or minor triads.

The most common seventh chord in popular music is the *dominant-seventh* chord, which is usually spelled with a note name followed by a 7 (as in G7 and Eb7). A group of dominant-seventh chords is shown in **Example 3**. If these chords look similar to the major chords in Example 1, there's a good reason—dominant-seventh chords have the same three notes as their major counterparts, with one added note called the *flatted seventh*.

TRACK 16 **Ex. 2**

(continued)

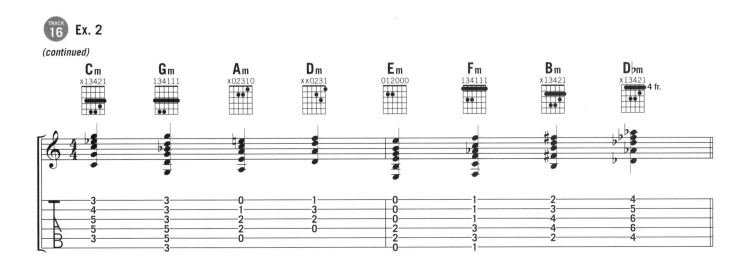

TRACK 17 **Ex. 3**

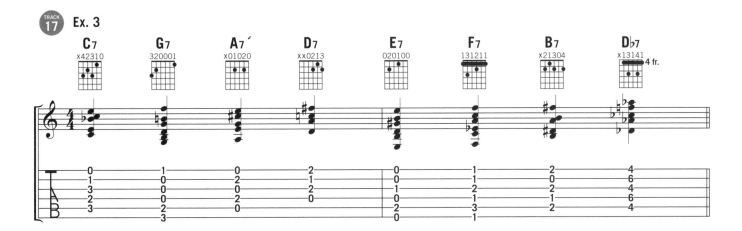

If you see a chord that looks like a minor chord and a seventh chord at the same time, trust your instincts—that's exactly what it is: a *minor-seventh* chord. This book uses shorthand like Dm7 and B♭m7, but other sources sometimes use abbreviations like Dmin7 and B♭-7. In any case, these are just like regular minor triads with a flatted-seventh note added. **Example 4** shows some common minor-seventh chords. Another common seventh chord is the major-seventh chord. In these pages we abbreviate this chord with *maj7*, as in Amaj7 or C♯maj7, but other widely recognized abbreviations include a capital *M* (like AM7) or even a triangle (like C♯△7).

These chords confuse a lot of players. After all, since the dominant-seventh chord includes the notes of a major chord, isn't it also a major-seventh chord? The answer is no. In major-seventh chords, the *major* refers to the seventh note. While dominant- and minor-seventh chords add a flatted-seventh note to the underlying triad, major-seventh chords

have a *major-seventh* note (one-fret above where the flatted seventh would be and one fret below the root). **Example 5** shows some easy major-seventh chords. Compare the Amaj7 to the A7 in Example 3 to see and hear the difference between these two types of chords. Major-seventh chords have a smooth, mellow sound that makes them sound right at home in jazz and pop music.

It might seem a little strange, but when you come across chord symbols that include *extensions* (numbers greater than seven—particularly 9, 11, and 13), you can usually get away with playing one of these seventh chords instead. If the chord includes a *min* or *m* (as in Dm9), chances are you can play a minor-seventh chord (like Dm7) and not ruin anybody's evening. A fully voiced Dm9 chord includes all of the notes of a Dm7 chord anyway! Likewise, extended chords that include *M* or *maj* (like Cmaj13) can be played as major-seventh chords (Cmaj7). If a chord includes 9, 11, or 13 without any additional markings (like F9 or F13), a dominant-seventh

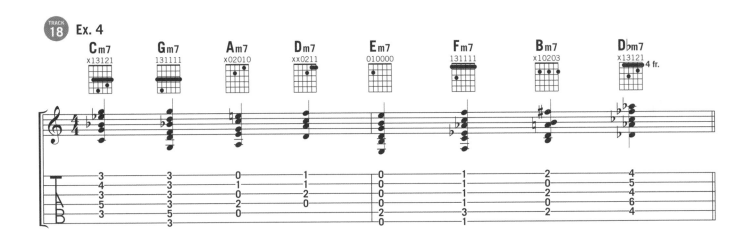

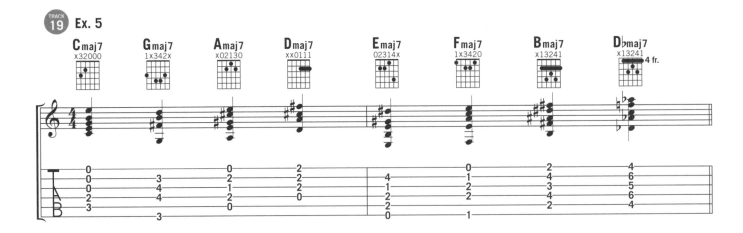

chord (F7) will sound fine. If you're backing up a lead instrument on a tune that includes these chords, the song's melody may very well include those extensions. That doesn't mean you should forgo learning to play other extended chords, but seventh-chord shapes make great substitutes if you're not quite there yet.

Don't Panic!

If any of the terms used in this lesson left you scratching your head, don't worry—you're in good company. But if you take the time to learn just a few of these shapes, you can actually play any

chord type no matter what note it's named for. Some of the shapes in Examples 1–5 are movable, which means you can shift them up and down the neck to make chords rooted on different notes. **Examples 6–10** (on pages 22 and 23) take these shapes and move them around to show each chord type in every key.

More Chords

The short list of chord symbols we've covered will allow you to play many songs, but it doesn't include every type of chord you'll come across. Take a look at the chart for some other popular chords and their symbols.

Other Popular Chord Symbols

SYMBOL(S)		CHORD
Csus Csus4 Csus2	**C**sus4 x3401x **C**sus2 x3001x	Any chord symbol that includes the abbreviation sus is a suspended chord. In a suspended chord, the third of the chord either moves up a half step to the fourth or down a whole step to the second. You'll usually see the sus followed by a 2 or 4, which indicates where the third is supposed to move.
C5	**C**5 x13xxx **C**5 x134xx	C5 stands for a C power chord, made from only two notes—the root and fifth. Rock music wouldn't be the same without 5 chords.
C6	**C**6 x42310	Add the sixth note of a major scale to a major triad with the same root, and you get a sixth chord. Add the same note to a minor triad with the same root, and you get a minor-sixth chord (like Cm6).
Caug C+	**C**aug x3211x	These symbols stand for "C augmented." Augmented chords include the root, third, and a raised fifth. The first chord in the Beatles song "Oh, Darling" is an augmented chord.
Cdim7 C°7	**C**dim7 x2314x	These are two ways to indicate a "C diminished seventh" chord. These chords include a root, flatted third, flatted fifth, and a double-flatted seventh. Diminished chords are rare in rock and pop music but can be found in blues and jazz.
Cm7♭5 Cø7	**C**m7♭5 x1324x	These symbols stand for "C half-diminished." Similar in construction to their fully diminished cousins, half-diminished chords (also called "minor-seven flat five" chords) include a root, flatted third, flatted fifth, and a regular flatted seventh.
Cm(maj7) C-Δ7	**C**m(maj7) x14231	A rarity! This symbol means "C-minor, major-seventh." Combine a minor triad with a major-seventh note to produce this oddity.

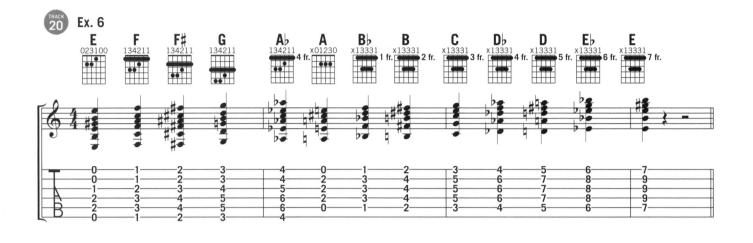

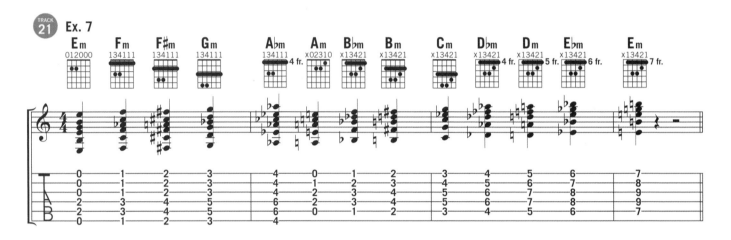

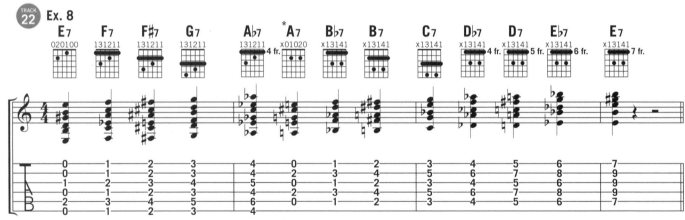

* **Six-string barred shape played on audio (same as A♭7, moved up one fret)**

22

TRACK 23 Ex. 9

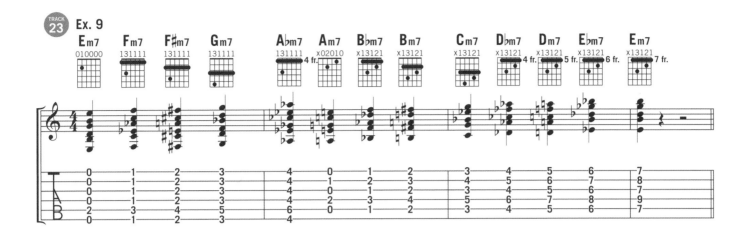

TRACK 24 Ex. 10

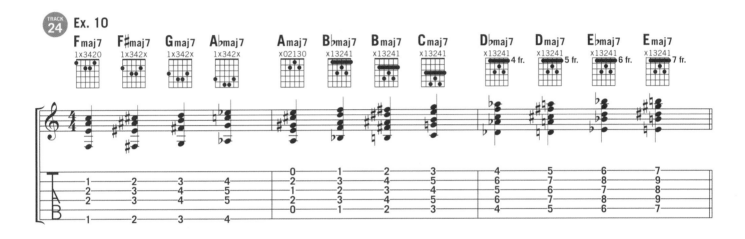

THE FUNDAMENTALS OF TIME

Ruth Parry

One stereotypical view of musicians is that we're always late. This is a little ironic because for us, at least in a musical context, time is a very important thing! Time is the foundation on which music is built and it's tied to a great number of concepts with which you may be familiar, including tempo (the speed at which a song is played), rhythm (durations and accents of notes), and beat (the underlying pulse as a unit of time). In this lesson, we'll discuss the ways in which musicians talk about time, explain why it's important, and offer some helpful tips on keeping it a priority while you play.

Take Some Notes

Any given note's rhythmic value (the amount of time the note should be held) is designated in sheet music by the note's shape, a combination of a note head and (usually) a stem.

Below is a quick reference chart outlining some of the rhythmic values you're most likely to see.

A quarter note lasts for one beat, or one tick of a metronome. A half note lasts for two beats, meaning you strike the note or chord and count to two before the sound stops—the same amount of time as two quarter notes. A whole note's sound rings out for four beats. In 4/4 time (the most common time signature in Western music), a measure is four beats long, so a whole note lasts for the entire measure. **Example 1** shows some quarter, half, and whole notes at work in 4/4 time.

An eighth note is worth one half of a beat; in one beat—the length of one quarter note—you can play two eighth notes. When people count eighth notes, they usually refer to notes that fall right on the beat with a number, and to notes that fall between beats with an *and*—two beats of eighth

Note/Rest Type	Note Shape	Rest Shape	Rhythmic Value
Quarter note	♩	𝄽	1 beat
Half note	𝅗𝅥	▬	2 beats
Whole note	𝅝	▬	4 beats
Eighth note	♪	𝄾	1/2 beat
16th note	𝅘𝅥𝅯	𝄿	1/4 beat
Dotted quarter note	♩.	𝄽	1½ beats
Dotted half note	𝅗𝅥.	▬.	3 beats

notes beginning on beat one of a measure would be counted one-and two-and. Meanwhile, 16th notes are worth one quarter of a beat, so you can play *four* 16th notes in one beat. Sixteenth notes are counted the same way as eighth notes, but with two extra notes thrown in—four 16th notes starting on beat one would be counted one-ee-and-a. In **Example 2**, you'll find a mix of eighth and 16th notes, along with some of the longer durations we've already covered. You may need to set your metronome at a slow speed to hit all of the 16th

notes—remember, you'll need to be able to fit four evenly spaced 16th notes in one click of the metronome!

A dot after a note tells you to add half to the original note value. For example, a half note is worth two beats; with a dot after it, it's worth the value of the original note (two beats) plus half that amount (one beat)—three beats in all. A dotted quarter note is worth one-and-a-half beats: the original value is one beat, and adding half its value gives us one extra half-beat. **Example 3** includes these note values as well as the others you've used thus far.

It's easy to forget about the importance of timekeeping while you're playing, especially when your attention is consumed by the pitches of the notes.

Rests are moments of silence in music. They have different rhythmic values, equivalent to note values. When you encounter any type of rest, you need to stop your guitar strings from ringing out, by touching the strings with either your picking or fretting hand. **Examples 4 and 5** provide you the opportunity to employ some of these rests in a musical way.

The Importance of Good Time

It's easy to forget about the importance of timekeeping while you're playing, especially when your attention is consumed by the pitches of the notes. But a steady focus on rhythm is actually as *important* as the note's pitch. Let's explore this idea by playing the melody in **Example 6**, which is in 2/4 time. This means there are only two beats in each measure (unlike Examples 1–5, which have four beats per measure), so you'll have to make a slight adjustment in your count to eliminate beats three and four. Is this melody familiar to you? Probably not. Now play **Example 7**, which has the same notes set to a different rhythm. It should be a lot easier to recognize

Example 7 as the melody from Beethoven's Fifth Symphony. In both examples the pitches are correct and are played the same number of times, but what makes the melody familiar is the rhythm.

When you make mistakes (and you will), have fun with them. Mistakes are opportunities to discover new and interesting colors in the music or create variations on the original melody. Play Example 8 and note the differences between it and the original melody in Example 7. You might think it sounds a little "off," but you may also be able to feel its relation to the original melody. Remember, this wasn't the case in

Example 6. In **Example 8** you're playing a different set of pitches, but the melody is still somewhat familiar because the rhythm matches Example 7. It's true that Example 8 includes some small differences, but changes in the notes and small alterations of rhythmic values can be fun ways to begin to explore and improvise—**Examples 9 and 10** offer some other possibilities based on the original melody in Example 7.

Six Tips for Keeping Steady Time

When people think of rhythm, they often think of a drummer, but the drummer isn't the only member of the band who has

TRACK 29 **Ex. 7**

(continued)

TRACK 30 **Ex. 8**

TRACK 31 **Ex. 9**

Ex. 10

to keep time. All members of a band have that job—if everyone does their part, listeners will say that a song sounds "tight" or "together." Here are some ways that you can learn to keep a steady, uninterrupted pulse. Try each of the ideas below using the melody in **Example 11**.

1. **Count.** As you get the hang of keeping the beat, it's a good idea to count along with the music as you play. You should count aloud at first, and eventually you'll internalize the rhythm and can count quietly to yourself. You may notice that when you hold a note for more than one beat (or during rests), time seems to slow down, but it's an illusion—time is still ticking away!

2. **Clap.** When you start to learn any new tune or when you're having trouble with the rhythm, put your instrument aside for a moment and count the beats aloud while clapping the rhythm. Separating the rhythm from the notes shifts your focus toward playing in time. It also gives you a chance to feel it in your body.

3. **Tap your foot.** This sounds easy, but it can be challenging to keep a foot going while your hands are busy on the guitar. It may take awhile to develop a steady foot. You can also tap your foot just during the sections that are the most difficult. Depending on the song, it might make sense to tap on beats two and four (of a 4/4 measure) or even beats one and three—whichever feels best to you should work fine.

4. **Sing.** Don't worry if the neighbors can hear you. If you know the lyrics of a song, singing them to yourself will help you keep the rhythm going. If you don't know the words (or if there aren't any) but you know the melody, hum it to yourself while you play.

5. **Look ahead.** When you encounter a rest or a held note such as a half note or a whole note, use this time to look ahead. When you ride a bike, you don't look where your tire is hitting the ground. Instead, you look out ahead of you to see what's coming and prepare.

6. **Slow it down.** When you slow down the tempo, your accuracy will improve. Play the melody once slowly and as perfectly as possible. Repeat this process, gradually speeding things up. Eventually the accuracy you have at the slower speed will stay with you at the faster tempo.

All Together Now

The short piece **"Paint by Rhythms"** sums up all the skills you've learned during this lesson and, I hope, will inspire you further! This music is based on part of a minor blues. Notice that the beats in the first measure don't add up to four—this is something you'll occasionally see in printed music, called a *pickup measure*. Don't worry; just play the phrase in time as though you were starting on the *and* of beat two. The subsequent measures feature variations in rhythm and pitch to give you more ideas about how to begin to improvise and use so-called "mistakes" to your advantage.

Be sure to apply the six tips presented earlier. Start with the second tip and clap out the entire example before you start playing, so you learn the rhythms before playing the notes.

Coming up with variations on a melody that last for the same amount of time as the original melody is a good way to start improvising and putting mistakes to use. As long as you play in time and come back to the original music at the right time, mistakes can provide new and interesting colors.

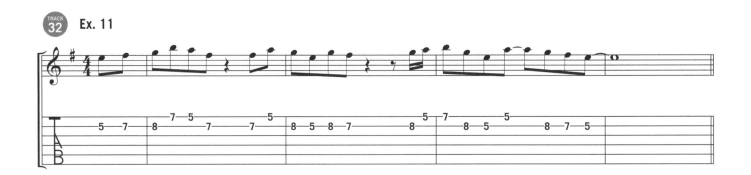

TRACK 32 Ex. 11

MUSIC BASICS FOR GUITARISTS

Paint by Rhythms

Music by Ruth Parry

 **Played up to Speed, then Played Slowly**

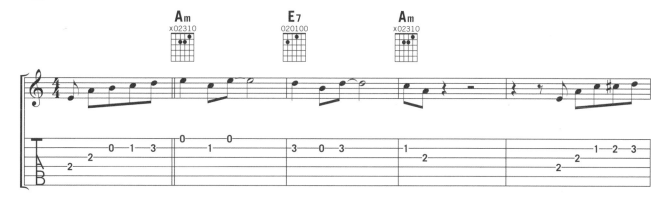

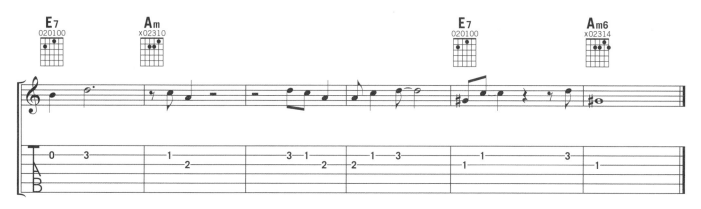

DIATONIC CHORDS

Dan Apczynski

Among the obstacles that confront beginning songwriters and guitarists, figuring out which chords "go together" can be one of the most difficult to overcome. For example, why does an E chord tend to sound out of place in a song with G, C, and D chords? Why do Em and G fit next to each other so naturally, while B♭m and G tend to sound lousy together? One of the first steps toward understanding how chords work is to learn about diatonic chords—groups of chords that are constructed from notes in the same diatonic scale.

In this lesson, we'll discuss how diatonic chords are constructed from the notes of a scale and the ways these chords complement each other—all of which will help you gain a better understanding of music, and even put you on the path to writing your own songs.

Construct Some Chords

To understand the concepts in this lesson, it's important to know your way around the basic major scale. **Example 1** shows a one-octave major scale in the key of C. These notes, from lowest to highest, are C, D, E, F, G, A, B, and C—the last note is one octave above the first. This is an example of a *diatonic* scale, but don't let the term scare you off—"diatonic" is simply a word that describes basic scales in Western music, made up of notes in a specific pattern of half and whole steps (think one- and two-fret jumps on the neck of a guitar).

What does this have to do with chords? Well, all basic major and minor chords are built from groups of three notes

(known as *triads*) that come from the steps of diatonic scales. Take a look at the following diagram:

C	D	E	F	G	A	B
I	ii	iii	IV	V	vi	vii

Diatonic chords are built by *skipping over* every other note in a diatonic scale. The C major chord (C) is built from the notes C, E, and G, while the D minor chord (Dm) is built from the notes D, F, and A. With just a little exploration, it starts to become clear how closely some of these chords are related—C and Em both have two notes in common (as do Dm and F, Em and G, F and Am, etc).

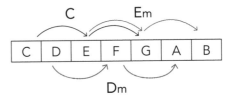

Major Discoveries, Minor Effort

If you're like many budding guitar players, you may be learning the guitar visually, so the notes that make up various major and minor chords seem less important than the shapes and hand positions that you use to play them. But chord construction isn't the only thing these diagrams are good for—they also give you some important clues about which chords fit together well in simple chord progressions.

Ex. 1: The C-major scale TRACK 34

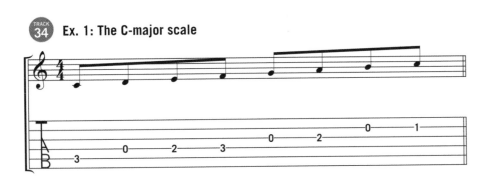

What's with the vii Chord?

The vii chord of a major scale is a pretty weird specimen—it sounds like a minor chord, but has one extra flatted note (the fifth). Called a diminished triad, the chord has a very unstable sound and as a result, tends not to find its way into diatonic progressions very often. Here are a few examples of minor chords and their diminished counterparts.

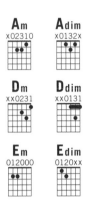

For one, the Roman numerals underneath each box indicate the major or minor quality of the chords built off each step of the scale. The uppercase I, IV, and V tell you that, in the key of C, we'll be working with major C, F, and G chords. Meanwhile, the lowercase ii, iii, and vi mean that chords rooted on D, E, and A will have a minor sound. This pattern of major and minor chords will remain the same in any major key—that is, I, IV, and V will always be major, and ii, iii, and vi will always be minor. The vii chord in any scale is something of a special case (see "What's with the vii Chord?"), but you can put the other chords to immediate use constructing simple tunes! Even just playing the chords in order offers a cool, ascending major scale sound, as in **Examples 2 and 3**.

Put Together a Progression

Just to change things up, let's look at a different key. Here's the same diagram as before, this time in the key of A:

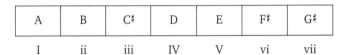

A	B	C♯	D	E	F♯	G♯
I	ii	iii	IV	V	vi	vii

Ex. 2: Diatonic triads (key of C)

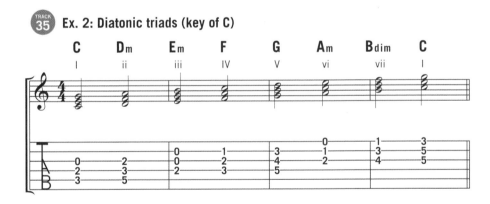

Ex. 3: Diatonic chords (key of C)

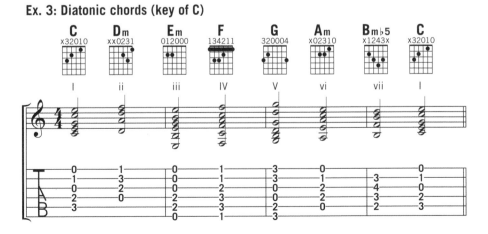

From the diagram, we see that the major chords in the key of A are A (I), D (IV), and E (V). Even with these three chords, you can put together some simple musical ideas, like the riff in **Example 4**.

But don't stop there—keep that idea saved and come up with another one. The ii, iii, and vi chords can help you change things up, and since they're in the same key, they'll fit

You can use diatonic chords as a shortcut to creating strong, sensible progressions.

TRACK 36 **Ex. 4: Diatonic progression in A**

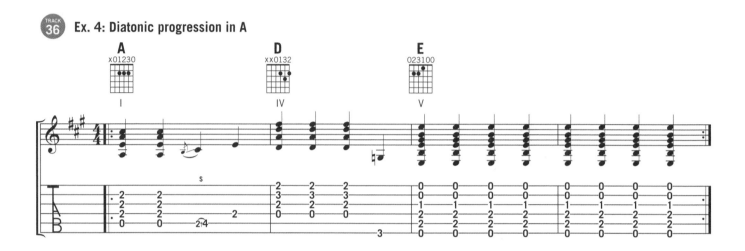

TRACK 37 **Ex. 5: Another diatonic progression in A**

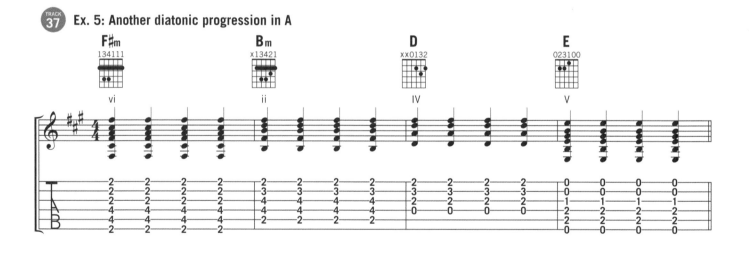

TRACK 38 **Ex. 6: Diatonic progression in G**

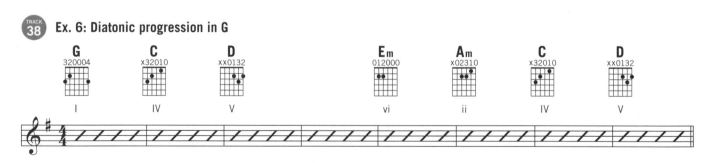

nicely with what we played in Example 4. Try **Example 5**, which starts on the vi chord (F♯m), moves to the ii (Bm), and then heads up to IV (D) and V (E).

We can also use this idea to transpose a progression to a different key. If you apply the Roman numerals from the progressions in Examples 4 and 5 to the G-major diagram shown here, you'll end up with something like **Example 6**. Since we've switched keys, the notes between chord changes (like the ones in measures 1 and 2 of Example 4) also have to change to fit the new key, but you can just strum the chords to get the idea.

G	A	B	C	D	E	F♯
I	ii	iii	IV	V	vi	vii

Now check out **"Dye and Tonic,"** which is an exercise almost exclusively made up of diatonic chords in the key of G.

While diatonic chords are great for writing simple progressions, it's important to note that songwriters also use *non*diatonic chords in their songs—often to highlight an important lyric or tweak their listeners' ears in just the right way. See if you can spot (or even better, *hear*) the nondiatonic chord in this song!

For further practice, here are scale diagrams for the keys of D and E. See what kind of progression you can create on your own.

D	E	F♯	G	A	B	C♯
E	F♯	G♯	C	B	C♯	D♯
I	ii	iii	IV	V	vi	vii

Dye and Tonic

Music by Dan Apczynski

THE CIRCLE OF FIFTHS

Adam Perlmutter

In the same way that visual artists use a color wheel to understand how primary, secondary, and complementary colors work, and scientists consult the periodic table to compare different forms of chemical behavior, musicians use the circle of fifths to help them understand relationships between the 12 pitches of the chromatic scale. First explained by Johann David Heinichen in his 1728 treatise *Der General-Bass in der Composition*, the circle of fifths can help you unlock some of the mysteries of music. (For handy reference, you might want to photocopy this diagram and put it on your music stand.) In this lesson, you'll learn all about the circle and its typical applications, both theoretical and compositional.

Find the Flats or Sharps in Any Key

The circle of fifths has a number of practical applications, one of which is determining how many sharps or flats are contained in a given key. The outermost "ring" of the circle shows which sharps exist in each key, while the next ring inward shows which notes are flatted. If you look at the outer part of the circle, starting with the key of C major (which is devoid of sharps) and travel clockwise, an interesting pattern emerges: each subsequent key has one more sharp. The key of G major has one sharp (F♯), and as you move around the circle another sharp is added (C♯ in the key of D, G♯ in the key of A, etc.). If you move counterclockwise, each succeeding key has an additional flat (B♭ in the key of F, E♭ in the key of B♭, etc.). The same principle holds for minor keys—shown on the innermost portion of the circle.

The circle also shows relationships between keys. For example, you can see that adjacent keys, like D major and A major, are closely related; they share all but one note—G♯. But as analysis will show, distant keys aren't even close—for example, D major and A♭ major, at opposite ends of the circle, share only two notes: G and C♯ (D♭).

If you want to know what notes are in a given major or minor scale, the circle can tell you. Each major scale has the same notes as the major key signature with the same root. For example, the A-major scale contains three sharps: F♯, C♯, and G♯. All of the remaining notes (A, B, D, and E), are played natural—neither

Major Keys

C
F
G
B♭
D
F♯
F♯ C♯
E♭
A♭
F♯
C♯
G♯
A
B♭ E♭
B♭ E♭ A♭
B♭ E♭ A♭ D♭
F♯ C♯ G♯ D♯
E
B♭ E♭ A♭ D♭ G♭ C♭
A♭ D♭ G♭
B♭ E♭ A♭ D♭
F♯ C♯ G♯ A♯ D♯ E♯
F♯ C♯ G♯ A♯ D♯
B
F♯ C♯ G♯ A♯ D♯ E♯
D♭
F♯ (G♭)

Minor Keys
D A E
G B
C F♯
F C♯
B♭ E♭ G♯

sharp nor flat. **Example 1** is built from the A-major scale harmonized in thirds. On the other hand, the circle tells you that the A-minor scale (which shares a section with C major) contains no sharps or flats. Remove the sharps from Example 1 and you're playing in A minor (**Example 2**).

You can also use the circle to travel between closely related major scales. In **Example 3**, to move from the G-major scale to the C-major scale, you simply lower the F♯ note to F♮.

Create Chord Progressions

The circle of fifths can be used to construct chord progressions. Take, for instance, the almighty I–IV–V, the basis of everything from "Twist and Shout" to the Ramones' "Blitzkrieg Bop." On the circle, start with any chord (which we'll think of as the tonic), go counterclockwise one segment for the IV chord (also known as the subdominant), and then go back to the tonic and move one segment clockwise for the V chord (also known as the dominant). A I–IV–V progression in the key of B♭ major, therefore, would be B♭–E♭–F. Play the I–IV–V

What Is a Fifth?

Simply put, a fifth is the relationship between two pitches that are five diatonic scale steps apart. This lesson deals with *perfect* fifths—the intervallic relationship between a key's tonic and the fifth diatonic scale tone, which are separated by exactly two-and-a-half whole steps (a distance of seven frets on a single guitar string). So, to find the fifth in any key, count the tones of a scale on one hand until you run out of fingers! Here are four popular guitar keys:

Key of C:	C–D–E–F–G
Key of G:	G–A–B–C–D
Key of E:	E–F♯–G♯–A–B
Key of Em:	E–F♯–G–A–B

Ex. 1

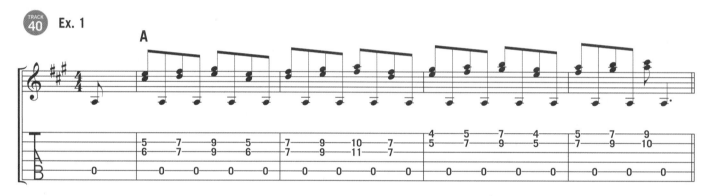

Ex. 2

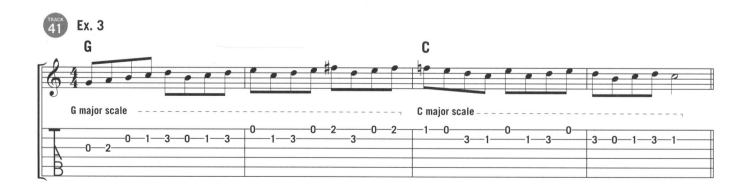

Ex. 3

shuffle in B♭ in **Example 4**, then use the circle to determine the I, IV, and V chords in various other keys. See if you can find the patterns for other types of progressions in the wheel.

An even more common harmonic progression in Western music involves the dominant chord resolving to the tonic (V–I). Try **Example 5**, similar to the eight-bar bridge of George and Ira Gershwin's 32-bar "I Got Rhythm," the basis of many jazz and pop standards. In the key of B♭, the bridge's progression is a chain of dominant chords (D7 is the dominant of G7; G7 is the dominant of C7; and so on) located adjacently counterclockwise on the circle. Note that the last chord of the bridge (F7) is then a V7 to the song's overall tonic (B♭).

As you've seen, the circle of fifths is a valuable tool for conceptualizing the fundamental relationships between keys, scales, and chords and can be used to sharpen both your playing and composing skills. For more practice, play through the fingerpicked étude **"Pickin' in Circles,"** the chords of which travel all the way through the major keys of the circle of fifths, starting and ending on C major. You can also try playing this piece backward (traveling through the circle of fourths!) to highlight the same dominant-to-tonic resolution shown in Example 5. To do so, simply start with measure 12 (or any measure, really) and play it from first note to last, then play the measure before it from first note to last, and so on.

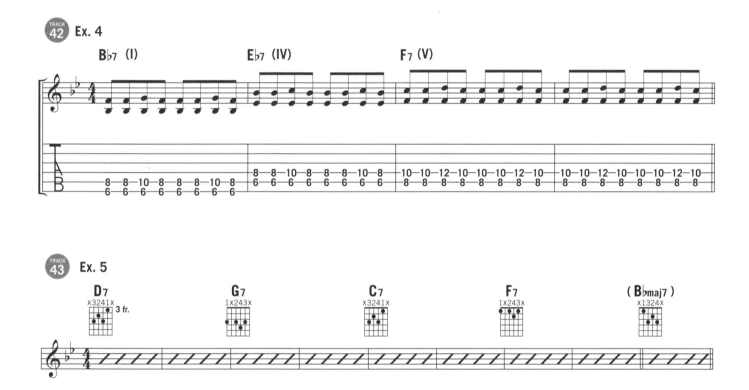

Pickin' in Circles

Music by Adam Perlmutter

 Played up to Speed

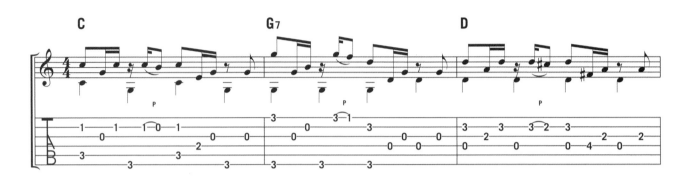

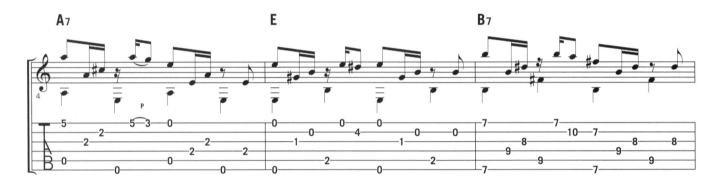

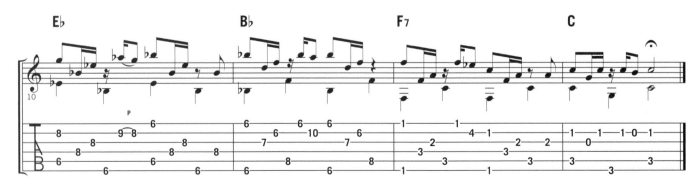

MUSIC BASICS FOR GUITARISTS

THE C-A-G-E-D SYSTEM

Dan Apczynski

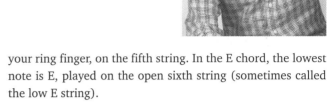

The open-position C, A, G, E, and D chord shapes seem simple by themselves, but used together, they make a powerful tool for learning and navigating the fretboard. The C-A-G-E-D system links these basic chord shapes (in that order), ascending up the neck of the guitar to create other chords—including some you already know. By experimenting with these variations (sometimes called chord voicings), you can add interesting new sounds to even the simplest songs. In this lesson, we'll give you the tools you need to play chords on the entire fretboard as well as some new ways to use chord shapes you've probably already learned.

The Open-Position Chords

If you're unfamiliar with basic, open C, A, G, E, and D chord shapes, **Example 1** shows the common ways to play them. These chord voicings are structured so that the *root*—the note each chord is named for—is the lowest note in the voicing. For example, the lowest note in the C chord is the C played by your ring finger, on the fifth string. In the E chord, the lowest note is E, played on the open sixth string (sometimes called the low E string).

Each of these chords is made up of just three notes. The C chord in Example 1 starts with a C note in the bass, followed by an E and then a G. The next two notes repeat the C and E notes an octave higher. If you don't yet know the notes of the fretboard, don't worry—every C-major chord includes these three notes, which are called the root, third, and fifth of the chord. They can be combined in any order to make a C chord, and since the fretboard includes many places to play them, there are many ways to play C chords.

Move Familiar Chords Up the Neck

Most experienced guitarists aren't content to stick to these first-position shapes—they play chords all over the neck. You can expand your playing by using these chord shapes in different places on the fretboard. Try taking the three-finger

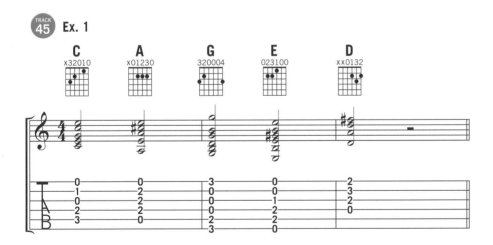

TRACK 45 **Ex. 1**

shape you used to make the A chord in Example 1, and move it up to the fifth fret (**Example 2**). This time, don't play the high E string. The result should be a somewhat exotic-sounding chord—you've moved the A shape up the neck, but the bass note didn't move with it. Your fingers are now on the G, C, and E notes—the notes that make up a C chord. (If you play the open A in the bass, the chord quality is different, sometimes called a C/A or Am7.)

Now use your index finger to bring the bass note up to the third fret, and barre the notes of the A shape with your ring finger (**Example 3**). This may be difficult if you've never played barre chords before, but with practice, you'll be able to make this chord sound as clean and smooth as any other. When you've got it down, compare the sound to the C chord in Example 1. If you're getting it right, the two chords should sound very similar. Both are C chords because they contain the same notes, but by playing them in a different order and position on the fretboard, the texture changes.

Build on the Bass Notes

Notice that both of these C chords have the same bass note (C, on the fifth string). If you think of these chord voicings as shapes—the C and A of C-A-G-E-D—constructed on these bass notes, you can use them to form other chords.

Example 4 shows a few ways to make new voicings of other familiar chords by centering shapes around different bass notes. The first pair uses the D on the fifth string as the bass, creating two new ways to play a D chord using the C and A shapes. When you move the C shape up the neck, you need to use your index finger to play the note that was an open string in first position, just as you did with the A-shape voicing in Example 3.

So far, all of the new shapes in this lesson have been built on fifth-string bass notes, but you can also build chords from bass notes on other strings. **Example 5** shows some of the possibilities of G-shape voicings. The first of these uses the full G shape from Example 1 (with the open strings now fretted by your index finger), and is nearly impossible to play—don't try

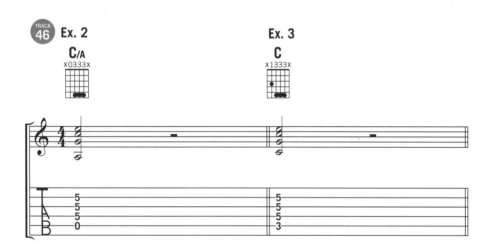

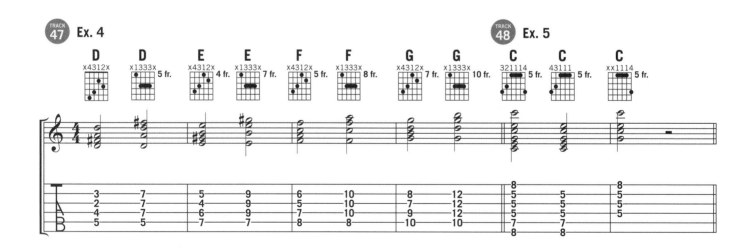

Know Thy Fretboard

Learning the names of the notes on each fret is an important step for any guitarist, but the bass strings are the most important of all. Use this handy chart to locate and learn the notes on the four lowest strings, and you'll be playing chords up the neck in no time.

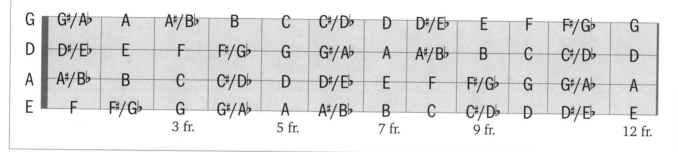

too hard, or you'll strain your fingers! The second shape in Example 5, built on the sixth-string, eighth-fret C, is a nice, low-sounding chord. The third shape uses just the top four strings, with a high C ringing on top for a bright, trebly sound.

Example 6 takes things even further, with—count 'em— five different voicings of C. If the last two look familiar, they should; their shapes are built on the E and D chord shapes in Example 1. We've now linked all the open-string chord shapes that make up the C-A-G-E-D system—C, A, G, E, and D.

Example 7 applies the same method to the E chord, although since we're not starting on C, it might make more

sense to think of the system as "E-D-C-A-G." (Not nearly as catchy, is it?) Play through these chord voicings and listen for the nuances of each one. There may be times when one of these shapes works better than another, so it pays to know them all!

The best way to internalize these ideas is simple: practice them in context. Take some familiar songs and substitute these new voicings for those you usually play. For a quick and easy drill, try the original tune **"Uncaged Melody."** Practice the chord changes slowly and carefully, and listen to how the melody floats along in each new voicing.

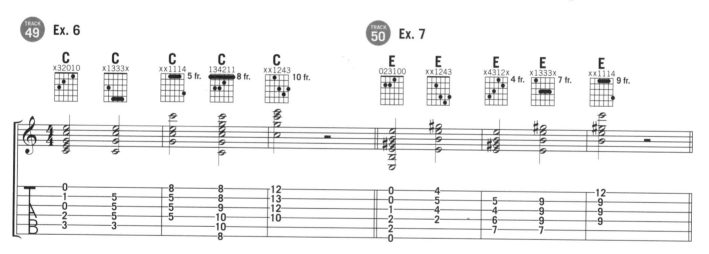

Uncaged Melody

Music by Dan Apczynski

Played up to Speed

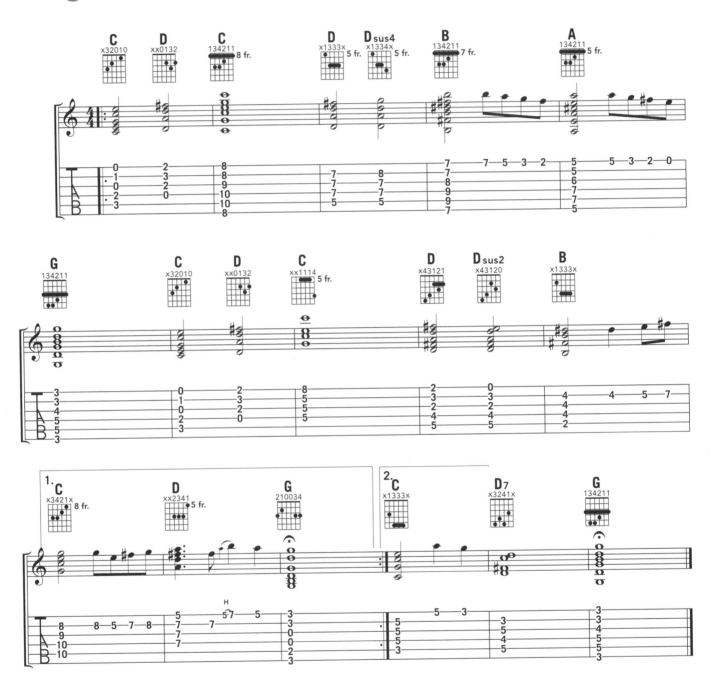

TRANSPOSING MADE EASY

David Hodge

Stop me if you've heard this one: Excited about learning a song, you track down the sheet music or tablature and plunge into getting every chord change, riff, and fill down as close to perfect as possible—only to find that you can't sing it in the key in which you just learned it. Your vocal range is just a little too high or low to make it sound good. What do you do? You *transpose*.

Many guitarists blanche at the idea of transposing, thinking it a dark secret that only the brightest of players could wrap their minds around. But the truth is that transposing is one of the easiest tasks a musician can do, and it's something that many guitarists do without thinking twice about it. By the end of this lesson, you will too.

How to Transpose

Simply put, transposing is changing a song from one key to another. This may sound complex, but it's as easy as playing a major scale. In fact, let's do that right now. The first measure of **Example 1** shows the C-major scale. Notice that the notes are not only designated by name (C, D, E, etc.) but also by degree number (1, 2, 3, etc.). In the second measure, you'll

> The ability to change keys so you can play or sing a piece more readily is one of the most useful skills in a guitarist's trick bag— and it's a lot easier than you may think.

find the A-major scale, also written out by both name and degree number. Playing scales like this is something you probably do all the time—and if you do, you're transposing.

When you transpose, you simply substitute your original note (in the original key) for the corresponding note in the new key. Thinking about the notes in terms of their scale degrees

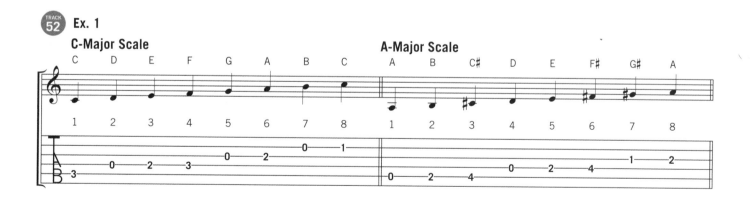

Ex. 1 TRACK 52

C-Major Scale — A-Major Scale

makes transposing as easy as secret-code games from childhood. Transposing from C to A (as we did in Example 1), C becomes A, D becomes B, E becomes C♯, and so on, through the scale. You can see that it's certainly not all that mysterious.

Guitarists find themselves needing to transpose chords more often than single notes. You do this in the same manner, using the numbers of the scale degrees (see "Easy Transposing Guide") to determine your substitution. **Example 2** shows a typical chord progression in the key of B. Let's transpose it first to C (**Example 3**). Because C is a half step higher than B, we're going to move each chord up a half step. The trick is to change only the *notes* and to maintain the *type* of chord—whether it's a minor, a seventh, an augmented, or a diminished chord. So B becomes C, E becomes F, F♯7 becomes G7 and C♯m7 becomes Dm7.

Let's try this once more, this time transposing it from B to G. Looking at the chart, you see that G is two-and-a-half steps lower than B. So we'll replace each of the B-scale degrees with the corresponding degree from the G scale. As you see in **Example 4**, B now becomes G, E becomes C, F♯7 becomes D7, and C♯m7 becomes Am7. Do this a few times and you'll soon be wondering what all the fuss about transposing was in the first place.

Easy Transposing Guide

Here are the scale degrees of the notes in each of the 12 major scales.

1 (the key)	2	3	4	5	6	7
C	D	E	F	G	A	B
B	C♯	D♯	E	F♯	G♯	A♯
B♭	C	D	E♭	F	G	A
A	B	C♯	D	E	F♯	G♯
A♭	B♭	C	D♭	E♭	F	G
G	A	B	C	D	E	F♯
F♯	G♯	A♯	B	C♯	D♯	E♯
F	G	A	B♭	C	D	E
E	F♯	G♯	A	B	C♯	D♯
E♭	F	G	A♭	B♭	C	D
D	E	F♯	G	A	B	C♯
C♯	D♯	E♯	F♯	G♯	A♯	B♯

Remember to transpose down whenever you can. To play in the original key when transposed, place the capo on the guitar one fret for each half step you transposed. If the original key, as an example, is B♭, and you transposed down a step and a half to G, then putting the capo on the third fret will have you back in B♭.

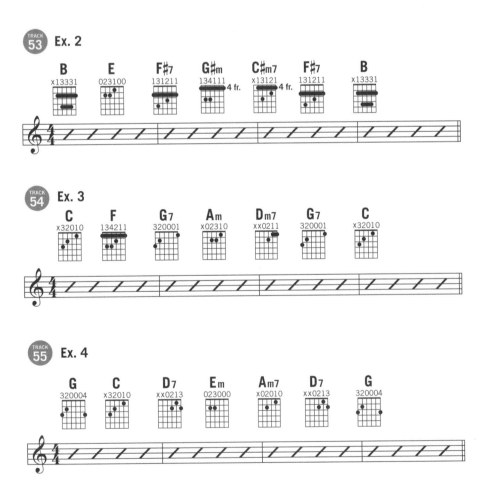

Transpose in Two Steps

There are all sorts of other reasons to want to transpose a song. Maybe your need to transpose has to do with vocal range (yours or another singer's), as noted earlier. By transposing, you can try out a song in different keys until you find the optimal one for your voice (or your friend's).

But what if the key you're comfortable singing in is E♭ or some other key that makes it tough to play the chords? In such cases, you want to use two steps: first, transpose the song into a guitar-friendly key; then, use a capo to bring the guitar back into the original key.

When doing this, it's important to transpose *down* to a friendly key, because placing a capo on your guitar *raises* the key. In essence, the two actions cancel each other out. In **Example 5**, you see a combination of notes and chords written in Fm. First, we're going to transpose them down a half step, to the key of Em. Then we'll put a capo on the first fret of the guitar, which raises the Em back up to Fm. When you play **Example 6**, it's going to sound remarkably similar to Example 5.

You can see that using these two simple steps made this example a lot easier to play. That is another benefit of transposing: You can often arrange to play a song with chord shapes and voicings that you're comfortable with. This is especially useful when playing in a group situation. If all the gui-tars are strumming open chords, the aggregation is going to sound fairly monotonous. You can add a little more spice to the mix by transposing a song—even if it's already in a key you can play in—to a key where you'll use chords (and chord voicings) other than the ones other guitarists are playing.

One Song, Three Keys

Let's try out our newfound skill with **"Broke and Hungry,"** an old blues song in the key of B♭. I've transposed it to three different guitar-friendly keys—A, E, and G—and given each version a different guitar part, so you can try out and hear the different voicings. The "A" guitar is playing a typical open-string blues shuffle, while the "E" guitar is using some typical blues riffs one usually learns in the key of E. The "G" guitar is playing some block chords to round things out.

Transposing, like any aspect of playing guitar, gets easier with practice. More importantly, it provides you with greater understanding of your instrument and opens all sorts of doors, both practically and creatively. With very little concentrated effort, you will go from writing out chord changes to transposing in your head. And you'll also develop a good feel for chord progressions and chord voicings, which will allow you to play by ear more. That's a great bargain for a small investment of your time and effort.

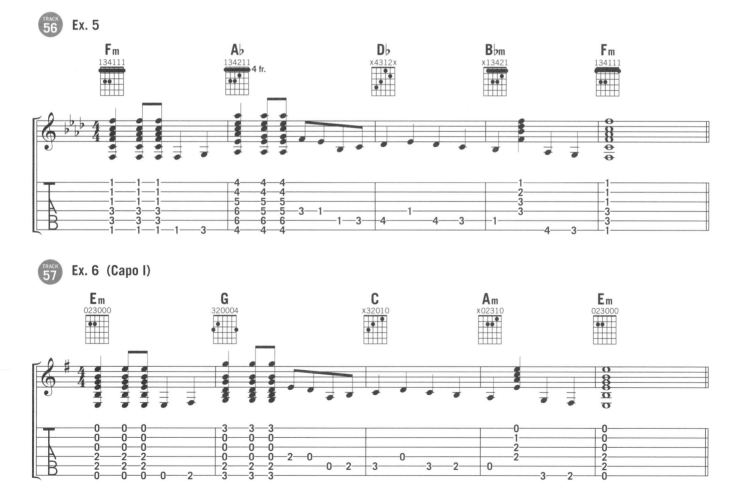

TRACK 56 Ex. 5

TRACK 57 Ex. 6 (Capo I)

Broke and Hungry

Traditional, arranged by David Hodge

(58) **Backup in A (Capo I)**

(59) **Riffs in E (Capo VI)**

(60) **Backup in G (Capo III)**

Swing (♫ = ♩♪)

Vocal Melody in B♭

I am broke and hun - gry   rag - ged and dir - ty   too _____

I say I'm broke and hun - gry _____ rag - ged and dir - ty   too _____   Ma - ma

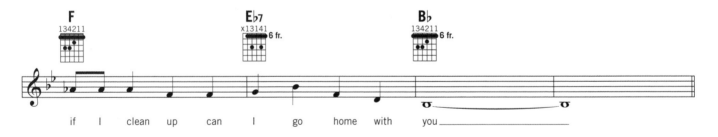

if I clean up can I go home with you _____

Backup in A (Capo I)

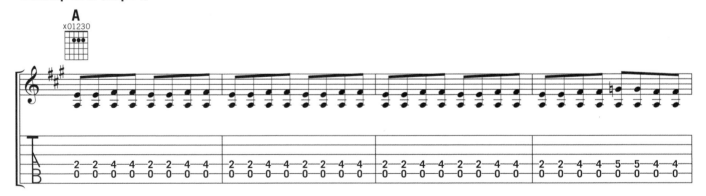

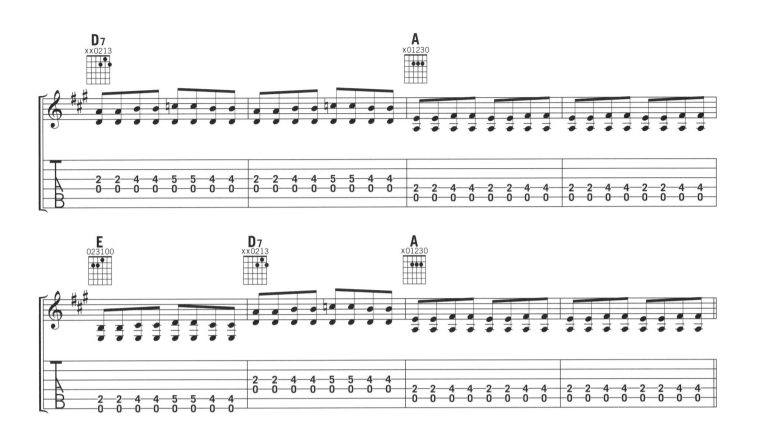

Riffs in E (Capo VI)

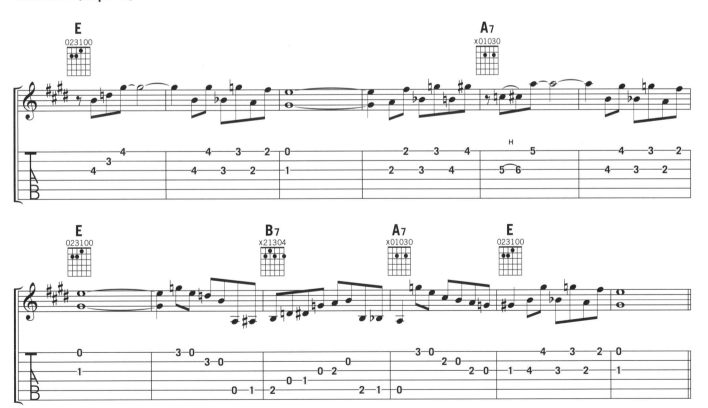

Backup in G (Capo III)

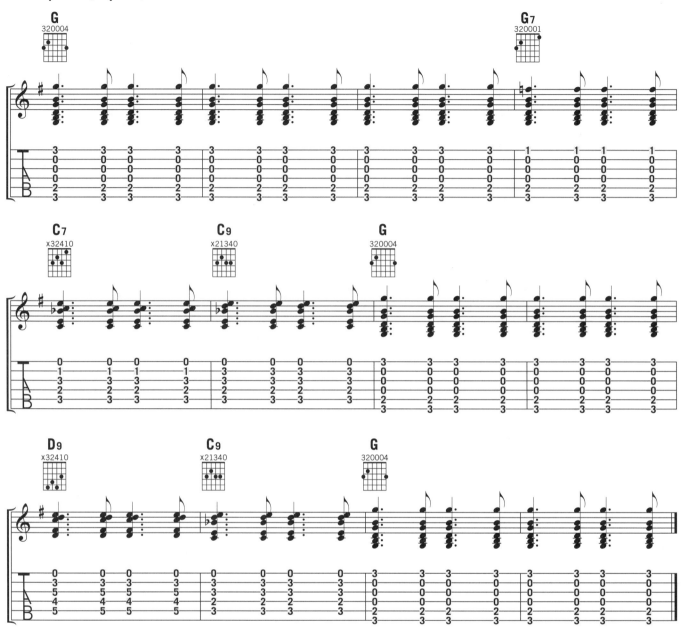

B♭
1. I am broke and hungry, ragged and dirty too

E♭7   **B♭**
I say I'm broke and hungry, ragged and dirty too

F7   **E♭7**   **B♭**
Mama, if I clean up can I go home with you?

B♭
2. I feel like jumping through the keyhole in your door

E♭7   **B♭**
I feel like jumping through the keyhole in your door

F7   **E♭7**   **B♭**
If I can jump through this time I won't ever jump no more

THE MAJOR SCALE

Andrew DuBrock

The major scale emerged around the eighth century AD but may have roots even further back in ancient Greek or Roman times. However the major scale came into existence, it has become the most important scale in Western music. If there's only one scale you ever learn, this would be the one to choose. In this lesson, we'll learn how to build a major scale in any key and discover how to find major scales all over the fretboard.

Building a Major Scale

You don't have to look any further than a piano keyboard to see how dominant the major scale is in our culture: the white keys spell a C-major scale. **Example 1** shows a C-major scale on the guitar, which uses the notes C–D–E–F–G–A–B–C. Play

up the scale a few times to get a feel for its sound, and then try playing the same notes in the reverse order. People often say the intervals in a major scale sound happy. An interval is the distance from one note to the next; a half-step interval is one fret, and a whole-step interval is two frets on your guitar. Compare the notation and tab staves of Example 1 to see the intervals in a major scale: whole–whole–half–whole–whole–whole–half. You can create a major scale for any letter name if you play those intervals in that order. **Example 2** shows a G-major scale (G–A–B–C–D–E–F♯–G). Notice how these C-major and G-major shapes are the same. You can play a major scale in any key by using this shape, as long as you start on the sixth string (including the sharped or flatted notes like B♭ and C♯).

Ex. 1: C-Major Scale

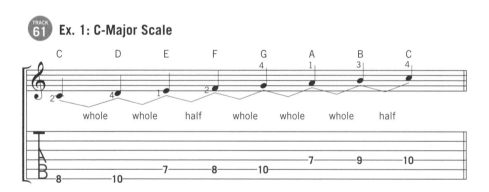

Ex. 2: G-Major Scale

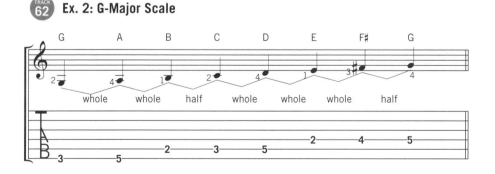

Going one step further, you can build any scale anywhere on the fretboard by following the whole- and half-step intervals we used in Examples 1 and 2. Try building an A-major scale, starting with your open A string (you can check yourself with **Example 3**). Here, you can see that building a major scale on A produces three sharp notes—C♯, F♯, and G♯—and a scale of A–B–C♯–D–E–F♯–G♯–A.

Major Scales in Multiple Places

The six open strings on a guitar all sound different notes across different registers, but when you play ascending notes up each one, those pitches eventually overlap with the playable notes on the next highest string. Because of this, you can play most notes in multiple places on the guitar's fretboard, which also means you can play the same scale in many places

on your guitar. For instance, the A-major scale from Example 3 can also be played in second position (**Example 4**), fourth position (**Example 5**), and fifth position (**Example 6**). Though it may be a little awkward, you can also play this same scale all on one string as in **Example 7**.

The A-major scales shown in Examples 3–7 are all played in the same *octave* (the distance between any given note and that same note in the next highest register—for instance, the difference in pitch between E on the open sixth string and E at the 12th fret). But you can play the A-major scale in other octaves, like the scale shown in **Example 8**, which is one octave above the previous scales.

For any given scale and any given position on the guitar neck, you actually have access to more notes than just a one-octave major scale; depending on the scale and the position,

TRACK 63 **Ex. 3: A-Major Scale**

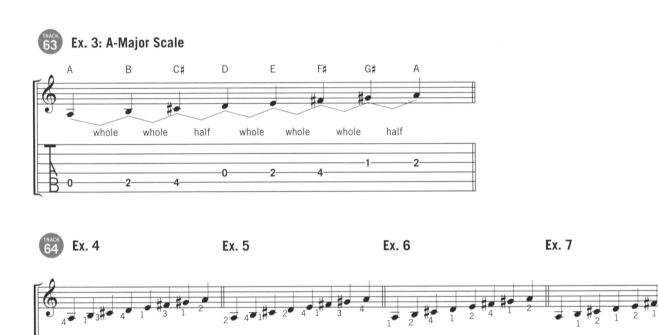

TRACK 64 **Ex. 4**   **Ex. 5**   **Ex. 6**   **Ex. 7**

TRACK 65 **Ex. 8**

you often have access to two full octaves of that major scale! **Example 9** shows how you can play a two-octave A-major scale in root position. You can also play two octaves of the A-major scale in second, fourth, and fifth positions (**Examples 10, 11,** and **12,** respectively).

Major-Scale Melodies

Running up and down scales is a great way to get them under your fingers, but it won't naturally generate great melodies. To do that, you have to add some creativity to those notes. Let's look at a few specific ways to help you get started.

> You don't have to look any further than a piano to see how dominant the major scale is in our culture: the white keys spell a C-major scale.

 Ex. 9

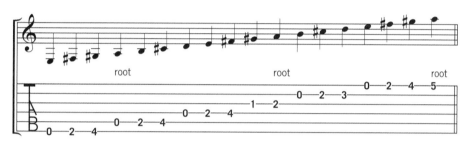

 Ex. 10

Ex. 11

Ex. 12

Running through small portions of the scale is a great way to start working on melodies (**Example 13**). The two downward moves in this line are just enough to keep it sounding less like a scale, and more like a melody. Another technique you can try is repetition—repeating a note, multiple notes, or a set of notes. **Example 14** uses a line similar to Example 13 and adds one small repetition—the G♯ note at the beginning of the second measure. Not only does this mix things up a bit, but it also allows the line to reach the final note on a downbeat, rather than on an upbeat (neither way is better, but it's a nice change).

One more way to create major-scale melodies is to leap around the scale (**Example 15**). This moves things away from that scale sound, but melodies start to sound a little broken if you use this method without any other. You can also create melodies by varying the rhythm. **Example 16** is similar to Example 15, but adds rhythmic variation by making some notes longer or shorter. Changing notes this way or adding rests between phrases is a great way to make your lines more interesting.

Of course, the best way to create melodies is to incorporate *all* of the above ideas (and anything else you can think of). For example, the opening melody to "America the Beautiful" (**Example 17**) has notes with varied rhythm (the dotted quarters and eighths), jumps notes several times (E to C♯ and E to B), and also uses a scale excerpt (B up to G♯) to

TRACK 68 Ex. 13

TRACK 69 Ex. 14

TRACK 70 Ex. 15

TRACK 71 Ex. 16

TRACK 72 Ex. 17: "America the Beautiful"

create a nice melody. American folk song "Tom Dooley" (**Example 18**) uses simple note repetitions and a few jumps, and varies the rhythm by adding eighth notes, half notes, and whole notes to the quarter-note lines (and even throws in a few quarter-note rests to spice things up).

Now let's see these techniques at work in the song **"Mostly Major Melody."** The first measure uses a small scale excerpt, a jump, and a little rhythmic variation to create a two-measure melody. I then essentially repeat that two-measure idea—with a few variations—three times to complete the eight-measure A section. The B section uses mostly small scale fragments. Again, I've crafted a two-measure phrase that I repeat with variations to fill out the entire B section. The A-section reprise adds a few nonscale notes to keep things interesting and a variation in measure 23 to accentuate the final ending.

 Ex. 18: "Tom Dooley"

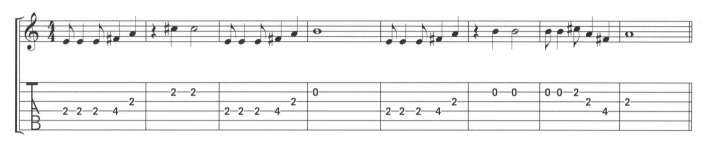

Mostly Major Melody

Music by Andrew DuBrock

TRACK 74 **Played up to Speed, then Played Slowly**

MINOR KEYS

Andrew DuBrock

n the heavy metal spoof *This Is Spinal Tap*, tortured guitarist Nigel Tufnel plays a song in the key of D minor, declaring it to be "the saddest of all keys." All kidding aside, while D minor isn't inherently sadder than any other minor key, there's still truth to the claim that minor keys are the sad ones. Why? The simple answer is that the chords and scales in minor keys highlight notes that our Western ears have become accus-

> Chords and scales in minor keys highlight notes that our Western ears have become accustomed to hearing as sad.

tomed to hearing as sad. Think about the intro to "Stairway to Heaven" or the melody to "House of the Rising Sun." Both songs are in minor keys, and they both have a melancholy tinge. In this lesson, we'll look at the structure of the natural minor scale (which we'll refer to in this article as simply the minor scale) and explain how the notes of minor scales work together to form the chords of a minor key.

The Minor Scale

Before we look at what minor keys are, we have to understand their foundation: the minor scale. **Example 1** shows a C-minor scale. Play through the example and notice how this sounds different from the C-major scale in **Example 2**. Look closely and you'll see there are only three different notes between these two scales: the third, sixth, and seventh notes. In the minor scale, all three of these notes are lowered one half-step. The sound of these three notes gives the minor scale its sad sound. To hear how they color a piece of music, let's

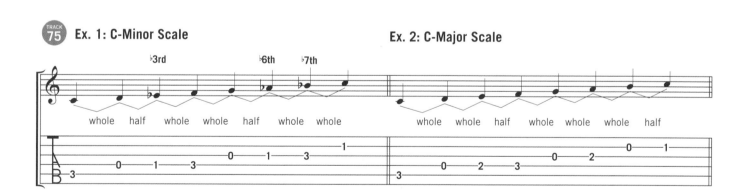

TRACK 75 Ex. 1: C-Minor Scale

Ex. 2: C-Major Scale

hear these notes in the context of a song. **Example 3** shows the familiar melody "Frère Jacques" in the key of C. Now play **Example 4**, which shows how this song would sound using the minor scale—big difference!

Look at Examples 1 and 2 again, paying attention to the *whole* and *half* markings between the notation and tablature staves. These indicate the distance between each scale tone. For example, the distance from the first to the second note is a whole step (a two-fret jump on a guitar), while the distance from the second to the third note is a half step (a one-fret jump). Any scale with the whole and half steps in the same order as Example 1 (whole–half–whole–whole–half–whole–whole) is a minor scale. If you follow this same pattern, you can start on any note and you'll always end up playing a minor scale. Likewise, any scale with the whole and half steps

arranged as in Example 2 (whole–whole–half–whole–whole–whole–half) is a major scale.

Chords for Minor Keys

As with major keys and their respective major scales (see the "Diatonic Chords" lesson), the most common chords musicians use when playing in a minor key are built from the notes of the minor scale of that key. **Example 5** shows how this is done. Each three-note chord (also known as a *triad*) is built using the steps of the A-minor scale. Notice how the notes of each triad stack evenly on top of each other, skipping a scale tone between each chord note.

However, notice the odd-sounding chord built on the scale's second degree. Chords like these are called diminished triads, and can actually be used quite colorfully in the right

 Ex. 3: "Frère Jacques" in C major

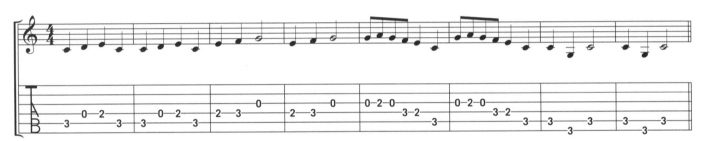

Ex. 4: "Frère Jacques" in C minor

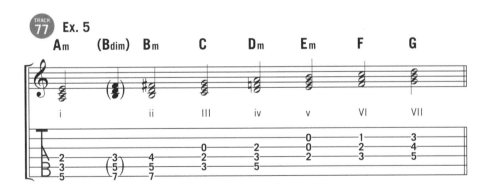

Ex. 5

MUSIC BASICS FOR GUITARISTS

circumstances. But in many situations, since a diminished triad sounds so strange, people use a minor chord here instead. There are lots of other chordal variations. One common substitution is to use a major chord on the fifth degree instead of a minor chord (which in A minor, for instance, would mean an E chord instead of Em).

Songs in Minor Keys

Now that we have a little of the theory out of the way, let's play some music! **Example 6** shows a common chord progression in the key of A minor (using the chords in Example 5). This progression (with chords built on the first, seventh, and sixth scale degrees) sounds a bit like the one used in Bob

Dylan's "All Along the Watchtower" and the guitar solo in "Stairway to Heaven." **Example 7** moves the same sequence of chords to the key of E minor, where the i, VII, and VI chords are Em, D, and C (respectively).

Now let's play the minor-key Turlough O'Carolan song **"Carolan's Welcome."** This piece uses nearly every chord in A minor (all except B minor) and every note in the A-minor scale. Don't let the notes up the neck in the B section intimidate you. If you slide up to the fifth position, with your index finger on the fifth fret, you should be able to grab all the notes in measures 17–21 without moving your hand. Once you reach measure 22, play the open E string on beat one and slide your hand back down to the nut for the rest of the song.

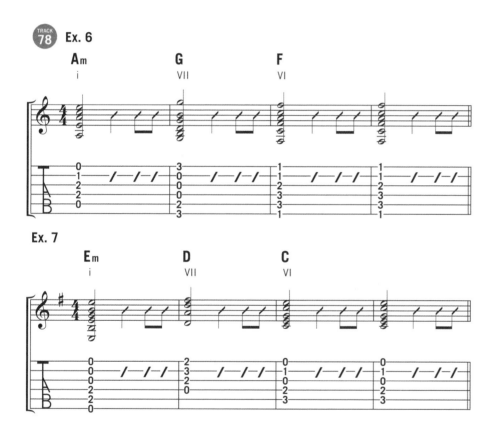

Carolan's Welcome

Traditional, arranged by Andrew DuBrock

 **Played up to Speed, then Played Slowly**

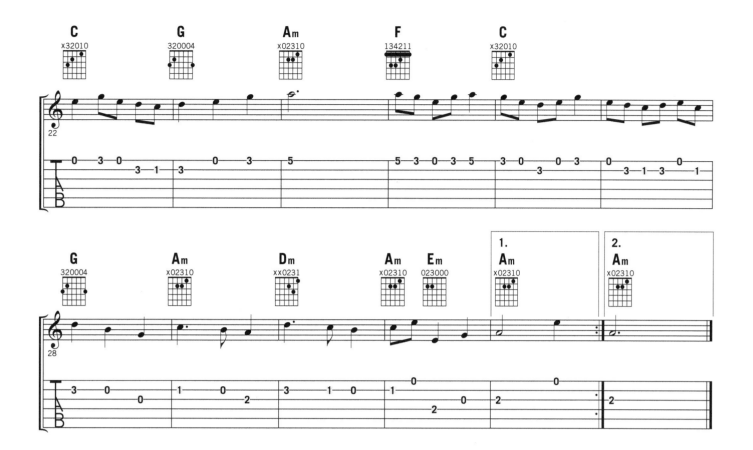

Major- and Minor-Key Relations

Where the heck do the minor and major scales come from? They come from the Greek major modes. If you've never heard of modes before, take a look at Example 2. The scale itself is a particular mode of C—the Ionian mode. If you start that scale on a different note—A for example—and play the same notes all the way up to the next A, you're playing another mode (in this case, A Aeolian).

These two modes—Ionian and Aeolian—are the most important modes in most pop and rock music. C Ionian is the same as a C-major scale, and A Aeolian is the same as an A-minor scale. Check out the following example to see their relationship at work.

Relationships like this exist everywhere in music: for every major scale (or Ionian mode), there is a minor scale (Aeolian mode) that shares the same notes. A minor is known as the relative minor of C major (which, in turn, is the relative major of A minor).

Not only do these scales share the same notes, they also share the same key signature. Here's a little cheat sheet that lists each major key, its relative minor, and their shared key signature. You can copy this chart and put it in your guitar case for reference, but you should also try to memorize these relationships, so you don't have to rely on it!

For more on modes—there are seven in all including Ionian and Aeolian—see the "Understanding Modes" lesson.

C Major/A Minor
G Major/E Minor
D Major/B Minor
A Major/F♯ Minor
E Major/C♯ Minor
B Major/G♯ Minor
G♭ Major/E♭ Minor
D♭ Major/B♭ Minor
A♭ Major/F Minor
E♭ Major/C Minor
B♭ Major/G Minor
F Major/D Minor

C-major scale

A-minor scale

PENTATONIC SCALES

Adam Perlmutter

Rock guitar instructors sometimes tell their beginner-level students that the minor-pentatonic scale is "all you'll ever need." While that's not exactly true, pentatonic scales—those made of five notes, as opposed to seven like the major or minor scale—are extremely useful. They can be heard in everything from folk music across all cultures to Western art music and American rock, country, blues, jazz, and beyond. In this lesson, we'll examine the construction and applications of the minor- and major-pentatonic scales used by guitarists of all stripes.

The Major-Pentatonic Scale

The major-pentatonic scale is derived from the major scale, but it's actually easier to play and memorize since it has two fewer notes! Getting there is easy: take any major scale (like the C-major scale in **Example 1a**) and play only the first, second, third, fifth, and sixth notes (the C-major-pentatonic

> Pentatonic scales can be heard in everything from folk music across all cultures to Western art music and American rock, country, blues, jazz, and beyond.

scale in **Example 1b**). **Examples 2a** and **2b** show two of the most common "box" shapes—two-octave forms within the same position—both for the A-major-pentatonic scale. Be sure to use the fingerings indicated, and play the scale both

 Ex. 1a: C-major scale   **Ex. 1b: C-major-pentatonic scale**

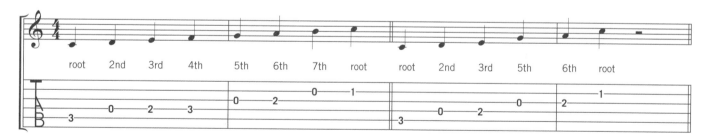

 Ex. 2a: A-major-pentatonic scale   **Ex. 2b**

ascending (as shown) and descending. Both are movable; you can shift either of the shapes up or down the fretboard to play in different keys. For example, move one of the patterns up two frets and you've got the B-major-pentatonic scale or down two frets for the G-major-pentatonic scale.

Many melodies you already know are based on the major-pentatonic scale. A lot of folk songs stick to pentatonic notes—"Oh! Susanna," shown in **Example 3**, for instance. The melody is written here in the key of A major, using only notes of the A-major-pentatonic scale shown in Example 2.

Pentatonic scales also feature prominently in the works of such composers as Béla Bartók, Claude Debussy, and Maurice Ravel. A well-known example is Debussy's piano piece "La

fille aux cheveux de lin" ("The Girl with the Flaxen Hair"), arranged for guitar in **Example 4** and transposed to the key of G. In this excerpt, the only melody note not in the G-major-pentatonic scale is the F♯ in the third bar.

In rock music, the major-pentatonic scale appears with far less frequency than the minor-pentatonic scale (which we'll get to in the next section), but the Allman Brothers made great use of this sweet-sounding scale in songs like "Jessica," "Melissa," and "Little Martha." Inspired by "Little Martha," **Example 5** features two-note chords from the E-major-pentatonic scales pitted against the open low E string, which you should let ring throughout.

 Ex. 3: "Oh! Susanna" melody

Ex. 4: From "La fille aux cheveux de lin"

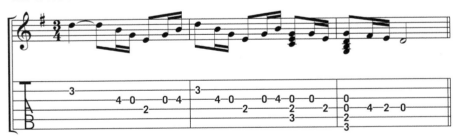

MUSIC BASICS FOR GUITARISTS

The Minor-Pentatonic Scale

Just as the major scale contains the notes of the major-pentatonic scale, the natural minor scale (**Example 6a**) includes the notes of the minor-pentatonic scale (**Example 6b**). The formula of the minor-pentatonic scale is different, though: it includes the first, third, fourth, fifth, and seventh notes of the minor scale.

Example 7 shows one common way to play the F#-minor-pentatonic scale. If this scale seems familiar, that's because it's identical to the A-major-pentatonic scale in Example 2, but it

starts on a different note: F#. If you take away the first note of Example 7, you'd have an A-major-pentatonic scale. Every minor-pentatonic scale has this same relationship with a particular major-pentatonic scale—to find the major, just start any minor-pentato1nic scale on its second note.

Minor-pentatonic scales are the most common scales in rock and blues music, heard in melodies, riffs, and solos. Contrary to its name, the minor-pentatonic scale is often used in major-key situations. This is especially true in the blues, since the scale contains two "blue notes"—the flatted third

 Ex. 5: Two-note chords from E-major pentatonic scale

 Ex. 6a   **Ex. 6b**

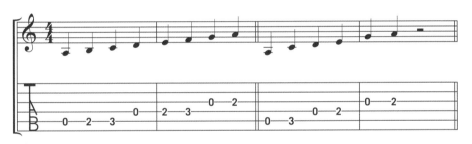

 Ex. 7: F#-minor-pentatonic scale

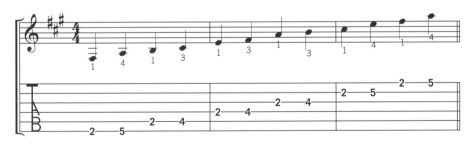

and flatted seventh, which lend a soulful character. But the minor-pentatonic scale is just as commonly played in a minor-key scenario. **Examples 8a** and **8b** contain an identical E minor-pentatonic riff on the bottom strings that works just as well in both situations—but notice that Example 8a is in E major and Example 8b is in E minor.

If you like the sound of the minor-pentatonic scale, you'll be glad to know that you can make it even more bluesy by adding another blue note, the flatted fifth. The resulting collection of notes (shown in **Example 9** in the key of A) is most commonly referred to as the *blues scale*. **Example 10** demonstrates how the scale can be used in a typical blues-rock application.

Unleash a Pentatonic Solo

The simple structure and shape of pentatonic scales are extremely useful for creating riffs and solos. **"All Pent Up"** is a 16-bar solo based on a I–vi–IV–ii (G–Em–C–Am) progression in the key of G major. The solo uses the G-major-pentatonic/E-minor-pentatonic scales for the G and Em bars and the C-major-pentatonic/A-minor-pentatonic scales for the C and Am bars, mostly in open positions. While you can play any of the notes in these scales over the chords shown, you can also use them to define each chord, as I've done. The lick in bars 9 and 10 is often heard in country blues and can also be used over an E or E7 chord.

Bars 13 and 14 contain a neat effect—natural harmonics are flanked by open strings to etch out the G-major/E-minor-pentatonic scales. Play each harmonic, indicated with a diamond notehead, by lightly placing a fretting-hand finger directly above the fret, so that when you pick the string you get a chime-like sound. Let the open strings and harmonics ring together, creating a harp effect. Feel free to borrow from the riffs shown here in your own improvisations! Once you've learned "All Pent Up" and understand how its pentatonic scales work, try improvising or composing some of your own solos and riffs using the notes of pentatonic scales.

86 **Ex. 8a: E-major progression with E-minor-pentatonic riff**

Ex. 8b: E-minor progression with E-minor-pentatonic riff

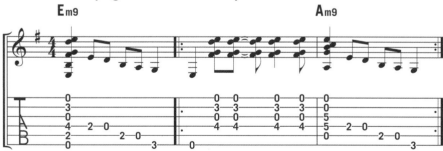

87 **Ex. 9: Blues scale in A**   **Ex. 10**

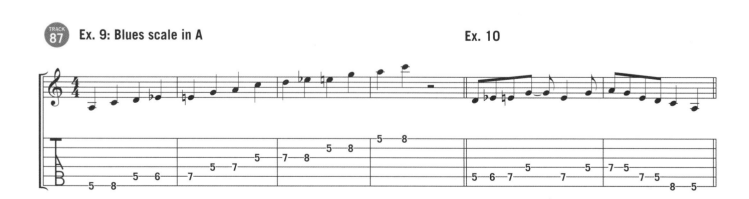

MUSIC BASICS FOR GUITARISTS

All Pent Up

Music by Adam Perlmutter

Track 88 **Played up to Speed**

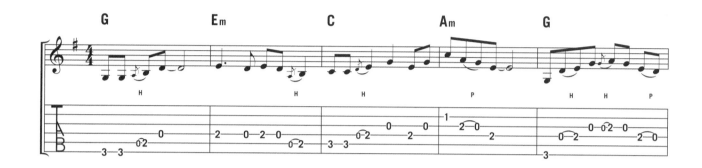

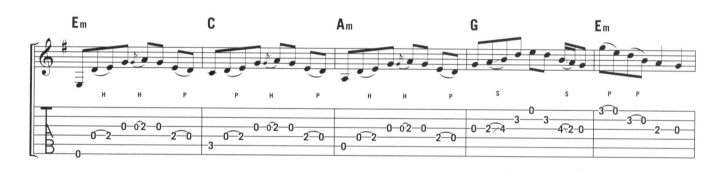

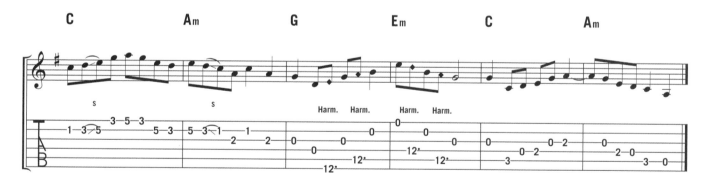

UNDERSTANDING MODES

Adam Levy

Most musicians are familiar with the major scale. You know, the old *do, re, mi, fa, sol, la, ti, do*. It's our elemental musical alphabet and the basis for melodies and harmonies in all sorts of music, from Bach to bluegrass. The scale's inherent character is sweet and consonant, and the music created with it tends to be agreeably cheery as well. If you're not sure what we're talking about here, pick up your guitar and play the G-major scale in **Example 1**—or check out the lesson in this book on the major scale. Got the sound in your ears and the feel under your fingers now? Make sure you do before we move on, because the major scale is the basis for all the other scales—the modes—we'll be exploring in this lesson.

The arrangement of whole steps and half steps gives the major scale its unique sound. As you may recall, the formula goes like this: whole step, whole step, half step, whole step, whole step, whole step, half step (sometimes abbreviated W W H W W W H). To build a major scale from a G note, for example, we'll start on the root G and go up a whole step from there (G–A), then up another whole step (A–B), then a half step (B–C), a whole step (C–D), a whole step (D–E), another whole step (E–F♯), and finally another half step (F♯–G). Strung all together, that's G A B C D E F♯ G—the G-major scale. To more clearly illustrate the W W H W W W H formula, let's play the scale along one string—the G string (**Example 2**). Keep in mind that a two-fret move is equal to a whole step, and a one-fret move is equal to a half step.

New Sounds, New Math

The major scale can, of course, be used as a vehicle for soloing, but it has its limitations. In looking for new sounds, there's no need to reinvent the wheel. There's already a solid system of alternative scales—the modes. The ancient Greeks developed modal theory, though our modern-day conception of modes doesn't strictly follow the Greek scheme. The modal system uses the major scale to generate seven modes, each of which starts on a different note of the major scale.

We'll use the G-major scale as our model. Building a scale from each of the G-major scale's seven notes, using only the notes of the scale, we get these seven modal scales:

G	A	B	C	D	E	F♯	G	Ionian
A	B	C	D	E	F♯	G	A	Dorian
B	C	D	E	F♯	G	A	B	Phrygian
C	D	E	F♯	G	A	B	C	Lydian
D	E	F♯	G	A	B	C	D	Mixolydian
E	F♯	G	A	B	C	D	E	Aeolian
F♯	G	A	B	C	D	E	F♯	Locrian

Let's examine these modes one at a time.

Ionian

The first mode is called the Ionian mode, which is synonymous with the major scale and shares the major scale's arrangement of whole and half steps—W W H W W W H. G Ionian is spelled G A B C D E F♯ G (**Example 3**).

89 **Ex. 1: G-major scale**

Ex. 2

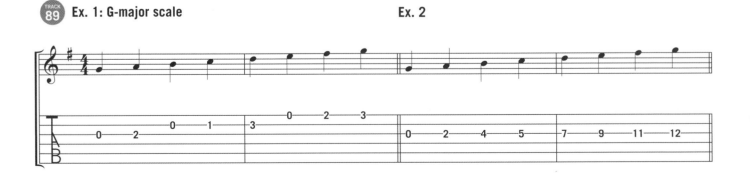

Modus Operandi

MODE	STEP FORMULA							SCALE DEGREES						
Ionian	W	W	H	W	W	W	H	1	2	3	4	5	6	7
Dorian	W	H	W	W	W	H	W	1	2	♭3	4	5	6	♭7
Phrygian	H	W	W	W	H	W	W	1	♭2	♭3	4	5	♭6	♭7
Lydian	W	W	W	H	W	W	H	1	2	3	♯4	5	6	7
Mixolydian	W	W	H	W	W	H	W	1	2	3	4	5	6	♭7
Aeolian	W	H	W	W	H	W	W	1	2	♭3	4	5	♭6	♭7
Locrian	H	W	W	H	W	W	W	1	♭2	♭3	4	♭5	♭6	♭7

Dorian

The second mode—beginning on the G-major scale's second degree, A—is the Dorian mode, spelled A B C D E F♯ G A (**Example 4**). Play the mode and you'll hear that it doesn't sound like a major scale, even though it contains the same notes. One way to examine a mode is to look at its step formula; the Dorian's is W H W W W H W. As you might expect, the Dorian formula is the same as the Ionian but is rotated so that the Ionian's first whole step is now at the end of the sequence. Another useful way to size up a mode is to compare it with a major scale starting on the same root note. In this case, that's the A-major scale (A B C♯ D E F♯ G♯ A). You can see that the Dorian mode has flatted third and seventh notes (C♮ and G♮, respectively).

Phrygian

Up next is the Phrygian mode, starting on B, the third of the scale. The B Phrygian mode is spelled B C D E F♯ G A B (**Example 5**), and its step formula is H W W W H W W. The B-major scale is B C♯ D♯ E F♯ G♯ A♯ B. Measured against the major scale, the Phrygian mode has flatted second, third, sixth, and seventh notes (C♮, D♮, G♮, A♮).

Lydian

Lydian is the fourth mode. C Lydian is spelled C D E F♯ G A B C (**Example 6**). Its step formula is W W W H W W H. The C-major scale is C D E F G A B C. Unlike the previous two modes, which diverge from the major scale by flatting notes, the Lydian mode has a raised note: the fourth, F♯.

TRACK 90 **Ex. 3: G Ionian mode**   **Ex. 4: A Dorian mode**

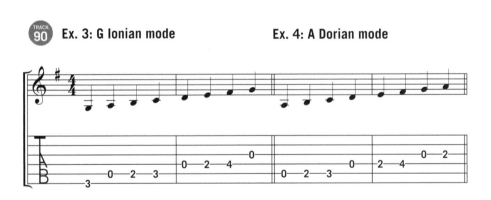

TRACK 91 **Ex. 5: B Phrygian mode**   **Ex. 6: C Lydian mode**

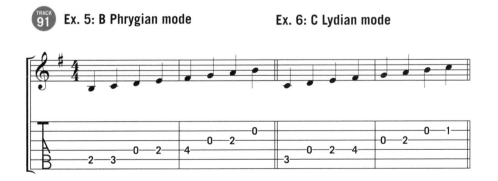

Mixolydian

The fifth mode is the Mixolydian. D Mixolydian is spelled D E F♯ G A B C D (**Example 7**), and its step formula is W W H W W H W. Compared with D major (D E F♯ G A B C♯ D), the Mixolydian has one flatted note: the seventh (C♮).

Aeolian

Next is the Aeolian mode. The E Aeolian mode is spelled E F♯ G A B C D E (**Example 8**). Its step formula is W H W W H W W. Compared with E major (E F♯ G♯ A B C♯ D♯ E), the Aeolian has three flatted notes—the third, sixth, and seventh (G♮, C♮, and D♮).

Locrian

The seventh and final mode is the Locrian mode. F♯ Locrian is spelled F♯ G A B C D E F♯ (**Example 9**). Its step formula is H W W H W W W. The F♯-major scale is F♯ G♯ A♯ B C♯ D♯ E♯ F♯. By comparison, the Locrian mode has flatted second, third, fifth, sixth, and seventh notes (G♮, A♮, C♮, D♮, E♮).

If you're having trouble digesting all this, you might want to copy the handy chart on page 67 and attach it to your music stand, bulletin board, or any other place where you can easily reference it.

Play Time

Now that we understand the math behind the modes, it's time to see how you can use these new sounds. That's the whole point, isn't it? The modes offer some very cool sounds to solo with, and each mode has its own flavor. But before you get your fingers flying, there's one more thing worth noting: modes are most effective for soloing in musical situations where the tonality doesn't move much—such as vamps that just repeat one or two chords. (Think of the solo sections from the Byrds' "Eight Miles High" or Santana's "Oye Como Va.") They can also be used over more complex chord progressions, but that's not their strong suit.

To get you soloing over each mode, I've provided seven simple modal vamps using A as the root of each mode (**Examples 10a–16a**) as well as suggested fingerings for the

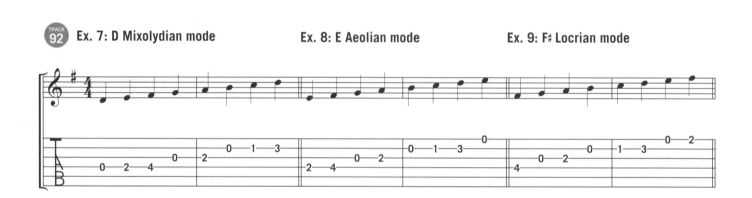

Ex. 7: D Mixolydian mode   **Ex. 8: E Aeolian mode**   **Ex. 9: F♯ Locrian mode**

TRACK 92

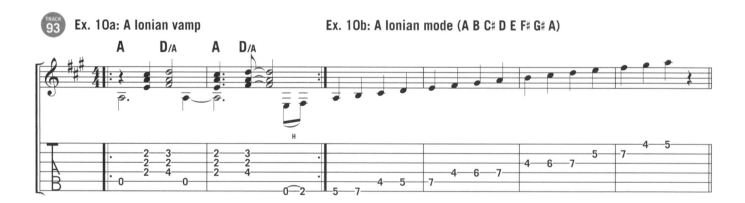

TRACK 93

Ex. 10a: A Ionian vamp   **Ex. 10b: A Ionian mode (A B C♯ D E F♯ G♯ A)**

modes to use for soloing (Examples 10b–16b). Play each progression a few times to get the sound in your ears. If you have a home recording device, record the vamp, repeating each example for a minute or two. You can then use your freshly made backing track to jam with. If you don't have a recording device, enlist a guitar-playing friend and take turns playing the vamps and soloing.

If you're new to soloing, don't panic—it's really not that hard. Simply experiment with the notes in the mode, playing just a few at a time, pausing for a musical breath, and then playing a few more. You may play them in consecutive ascending or descending order, jump around, or do a bit of both.

Generally, you'll want to spend most of your soloing time on the higher strings; melodies played on the bass strings can sometimes get lost in the mix.

Remember, each mode is really just a major scale in disguise. When you're using modes for improvisation, though, try not to think of them as "major scales starting on the wrong note." You'll get the most out of each mode if you can hear the mode's root note as its home base. True, you're still working with the elemental *do, re, mi*. But thinking modally, you'll go places Julie Andrews' character in *The Sound of Music* never dreamed of.

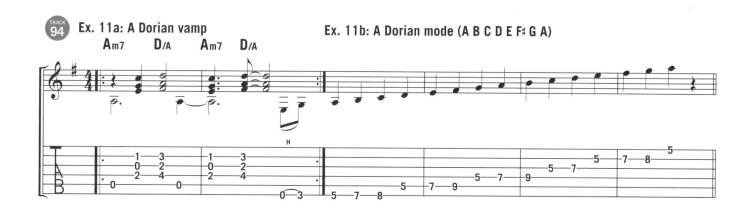

TRACK 94 **Ex. 11a: A Dorian vamp**   **Ex. 11b: A Dorian mode (A B C D E F♯ G A)**

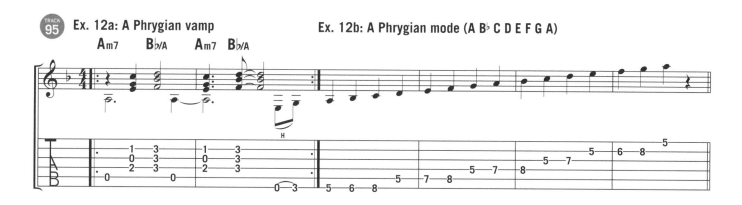

TRACK 95 **Ex. 12a: A Phrygian vamp**   **Ex. 12b: A Phrygian mode (A B♭ C D E F G A)**

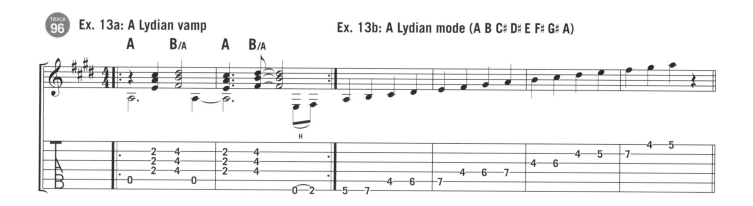

TRACK 96 **Ex. 13a: A Lydian vamp**   **Ex. 13b: A Lydian mode (A B C♯ D♯ E F♯ G♯ A)**

TRACK 97 **Ex. 14a: A Mixolydian vamp**   **Ex. 14b: A Mixolydian mode (A B C♯ D E F♯ G A)**

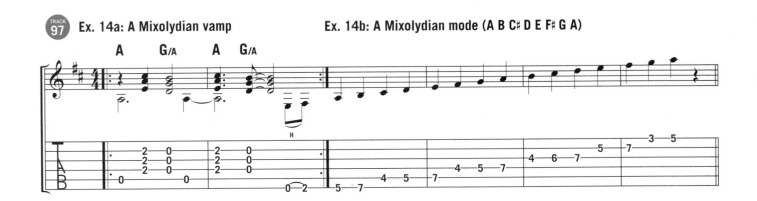

TRACK 98 **Ex. 15a: A Aeolian vamp**   **Ex. 15b: A Aeolian mode (A B C D E F G A)**

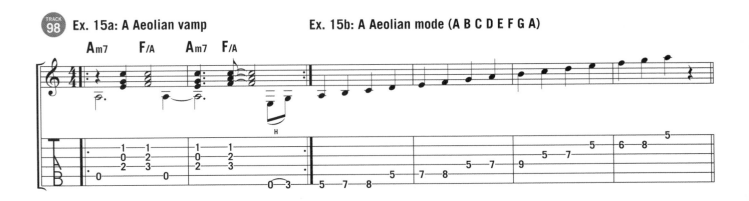

TRACK 99 **Ex. 16a: A Locrian vamp**   **Ex. 16b: A Locrian mode (A B♭ C D E♭ F G A)**

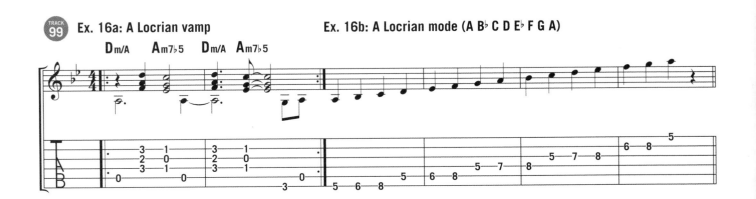

ABOUT THE TEACHERS

DAN APCZYNSKI

Dan Apczynski is an associate editor at *Acoustic Guitar* magazine. In 2002, he completed his bachelor's degree in philosophy and left his home state of Michigan for the San Francisco Bay Area, where he now thinks deep thoughts about music notation. When not engraving lessons for *Acoustic Guitar*, he gigs regularly around the Bay Area.

ANDREW DuBROCK

Andrew DuBrock transcribes, edits, and engraves music for print and multimedia publications. His clients include *Acoustic Guitar*, Homespun, Alfred, Hal Leonard, and independent musicians like Alex de Grassi and Michelle Shocked. DuBrock was *Acoustic Guitar*'s music editor from 1999 to 2007. He missed the gang so much that he pestered them until they parked his name on the masthead as a contributing editor. DuBrock lives in Portland, Oregon, with his wife and children.

DAVID HODGE

David Hodge has for years provided backup to numerous Berkshire County, Massachusetts, singer-songwriters. But teaching music is his first love. In addition to his private students, he teaches group guitar lessons for Berkshire Community College, and guitar students of all ages and levels from more than 168 countries read his lessons at Guitar Noise (guitarnoise.com). He is the author of *The Complete Idiot's Guide to Playing Bass Guitar* (Alpha Books).

ADAM LEVY

As a longstanding member of Norah Jones' Handsome Band, Adam Levy's electric and acoustic guitar work can be heard in cafés worldwide. Of his own jazz-tinged recordings, *Loose Rhymes—Live on Ludlow Street* (Lost Wax, lostwaxmusic.com) marks his debut as a performing songwriter. Levy's instructional DVD *Play the Right Stuff: Creating Great Guitar Parts* is available from Alfred Publishing (alfred.com). For more information, visit adamlevy.com.

SEAN McGOWAN

Based in Denver, Sean McGowan is a fingerstyle jazz and acoustic guitarist who combines diverse influences with unconventional techniques to create a broad palette of textures within his compositions and arrangements for solo guitar. His first recording, *River Coffee*, was featured on BBC radio, and he's had music published in Mel Bay's *Master Anthology of Fingerstyle Guitar*, Vol. 3. His recording *Indigo* is a collection of jazz standards and originals for solo archtop guitar. A regular contributor to *Acoustic Guitar* magazine, McGowan teaches guitar, theory, and improvisation at the University of Colorado–Denver. Visit him on the Web at maplesugarmusic.com.

ADAM PERLMUTTER

Adam Perlmutter is a freelance music transcriber and writer living in Brooklyn, New York. As a senior editor of *Guitar One* magazine and music editor of *Guitar World Acoustic*, he transcribed and arranged hundreds of songs; wrote numerous instructional pieces and gear reviews; and interviewed such leading guitarists as Jim Hall, Al Di Meola, and John Pizzarelli for both lessons and features. He has also authored several guitar-method books for Cherry Lane and Hal Leonard and can often be found lusting after vintage archtops he cannot afford.

RUTH PARRY

Guitarist/vocalist Ruth Parry has been a performing and recording musician for over 20 years. A graduate of Berklee College of Music in Boston, she has worked as a songwriter, composer, and arranger in a variety of musical styles and contexts, including the independent film *Jerome* by JET Productions, and has performed with Afro-Peruvian musical greats David Pinto, Marina Lavalle, and Lalo Izquierdo. She is also a guitar instructor at the String Letter Music School in San Anselmo, California.